THE LIGHT YOKE

DEBUNKING BANKING
HOW TO
REMOVE THE HEAVY BURDEN
OF BANK DEBT
WITH DIVIDEND PAYMENTS
TO ALL CITIZENS

BY
MESSIANIC MINISTER
KEN B. (MALAKAI) YEOMANS.

THE LIGHT YOKE

ISBN - 978-0-9808411-0-7

Published by:
Keyline Designs
P.O. Box 3289
Australia Fair Southport,
Queensland, 4215 AUSTRALIA.
Email: ken.yeomans@keyline.com.au
Mobile: +61 4 1874 5120
Skype: kenyeomans
Phone   +61 7 5591 6281
Internet: www.keyline.com.au

"Keyline" is a Registered Trade Mark
"Keyline Designs" is a Registered Business Name of Ken B. Yeomans.

Cover design by
www.logologologo.com.au

THE LIGHT YOKE

Biography - Ken B. Yeomans H.D.A.

Ken Yeomans is a fifth generation Australian, born in Sydney in 1947, becoming the youngest of the three sons of "P.A." and Rita Yeomans. Two years after his father's death in 1984, Ken established Keyline Designs, a rural property design and sustainable agricultural consulting business of which he is the principal consultant.

Ken and his wife of over 20 years Robyn are both ordained messianic ministers who lead Beit Gan-Eden Messianic Community, which they established in 1999. www.bgemc.org.

In the early 1980s, Ken, through a providential series of events, beyond the scope of this account, received a steady supply of literature and recordings on Social Credit, practical Christianity, banking, world government and secret societies that combined to provide the foundation for the understanding and proposals in this book.

In 1993, Ken published his first book, titled "Water for Every Farm – Yeomans Keyline Plan". It is available in Australia at www.keyline.com.au and overseas through Create Space, Amazon and Kindle. It is a recommended text for Permaculture students, rural landowners and property developers. In this book, Ken blended his own experience as an agricultural consulting engineer into various key sections he selected from the original four Keyline books, written and published by his late father P. A. Yeomans between 1954 and 1971.

Ken graduated from Hawkesbury Agricultural College, Richmond N.S.W. in 1969 with a Hawkesbury Diploma of Agriculture (H.D.A.). Ken Yeomans was a foundation member of the Agricultural Technologists of Australasia and is a member of the Irrigation Association of Australia and the Biological Farmers of Australia. Ken has a consulting practice in property design and development. This work includes the site selection, survey and plan preparation of earthworks for large farm dams and Keyline gravity irrigation systems as well as assessing and making recommendations on; rebuilding the living fertility of soil, grazing management, cultivation practices, cropping programs and subdivision design. Throughout the states of Australia and overseas, for clients with land holdings ranging in size from under four hectares to over four hundred thousand hectares, Ken Yeomans has applied his knowledge and experience of Keyline on family farms, multiple occupancy communities and rural stations held by large corporations.

Ken's interest in finance, economics and politics came from his father, who did not like the manipulative way banks could arbitrarily control the money supply and he had little time for socialism and its governments. This all became personal after Rita Yeomans died in 1964. Probate duties at the time were 50% of a deceased person's estate. Then the bank arbitrarily halved the business' overdraft limit severely restricted access to money as bank credit. These policies forced the immediate sale of the family's agricultural equipment manufacturing business and shortly thereafter, the sale of several of the original showpiece Keyline beef cattle properties near Sydney.

Introduction

The cost burden of servicing bank debt becomes a heavy yoke on all societies that accept commercial trading bank credit as a valid addition to their money supply. In 1978 the Bank of New South Wales revealingly published that: "All money is a debt of the banking system." In other words, the commercial trading banks create and issue all money. They claim this new money as their own and lend it at interest to borrowers. We are in effect using a rented money supply and there can be no end to the resulting debt.

The central problem identified and addressed in this publication is the claim by the bankers to own, issue and control all new money. The creation of new money occurs when banks authorize *additional* bank deposits. *Additional* bank deposits result from new bank loans and other bank purchases. *Additional* deposits expand the money supply and the debt. Transfers of existing deposits between bank customers do not result in additional deposits and so do not alter either the total money supply or total debt.

It is impossible to reduce total debt with borrowed money. We need a way to repay and thus cancel bank debt, without borrowing more money. To some extent foreign income achieves this. Foreign income does result in additional deposits yet no additional local debt. This precisely explains government enthusiasm for exports, tourists and foreign investment. Foreign investment is an euphemism for the sale of assets to foreigners. Foreign income is only a temporary fix. A lasting solution requires a better understanding of our situation.

Currently there are only three sources of money that can be used to repay bank debt. These are: new bank loans, current deposits and cash.

New bank loans are commonly used to repay existing bank debts; but bank credit is borrowed into existence, so it automatically creates a matching debt, which makes it impossible for bank issued credit to ever reduce total debt.

Banks allegedly re-lend most of their deposits. The proportion not lent is supposedly, their reserve. This can be expressed as a ratio; a fractional reserve ratio. The higher the ratio the less is available to lend. Governments can and traditionally have stipulated reserve ratios and in what form such reserve funds must be held. As a first step then, to significantly restrict the creation of more bank debt, the practice of so called fractional reserve banking must be progressively eliminated. This can easily be done by raising the fractional reserve ratio requirement. This move will progressively restrict banks from creating new money but will leave only existing deposits and cash to repay current bank debts.

Clearly a new supply of money must be created and put into circulation to replace the money consumed in the ongoing repayment of bank debt. A simple and undeniably fair way to maintain a stable money supply (money stock) whilst at the same time paying down existing bank debt will be to give to all citizens a fair share of new money as it is issued. The new money will be issued and distributed at approximately the same rate as total bank debt is repaid. In effect the new money will replace bank issued credit, which will be phased out of circulation. The interest charges associated with bank issued credit will then cease to exist.

The process of freely issuing money that is debt free, interest free and tax free to all citizens will avert any contraction in the economy whilst bank debt is eliminated. This additional supply of money will be backed by faith in the social credit of the community.

The new money will prevent existing cash and deposits needlessly being consumed by the repayment of bank debts. Commercial trading bank loans created the debts in the first place.

Raising the fractional reserve ratio will prevent the banks independently using the new money as an excuse to create and issue more bank credit, which would expand the money supply and cause inflation.

In Australia, Reserve Bank figures help show that the money supply and associated bank debts are around $60,000 per person. In other words, about $60,000 is your legitimate equal share of new money that will need to be issued to all citizens during the process of repaying total bank debt.

This book reveals in simple terms a viable alternative to the present debt based money system, which currently offers; inflation, unstable living standards, depression, debt bondage, war, environmental destruction and premature death to most of mankind and the illusion of power, wealth and luxury to a selfish few.

The problem is the continued licencing of commercial trading banks to issue and control all new money. The writer believes that the ownership of all new money issued in Australia, must be resolved in favour of every individual Australian citizen.

Some of the new money should also be used to fund consumer subsidies on local products.

Consumer subsidies can control inflation without the dreaded raising of interest rates and also make local products more competitive against the flood of imports from low wage and slave wage states or from countries that subsidise exports.

1. Money Making Unveiled.

The nerve centres of modern financial systems are the trading banks and the central banks they created to protect themselves, both from each other and the general community.

Trading banks have unique licences that are significantly different from that of other financial institutions; such as savings and loan societies, merchant banks, building societies and other, so called non-bank financial institutions.   The historical difference between bank and non-bank financial institutions is that trading banks can allow overdrafts of their customers' accounts whereas non trading banks can't.

However, modern banking institutions are, in practice, little more than society's bookkeepers.   Their legitimate role is somewhat demonstrated in the Parker Brothers' board game; Monopoly.

In the game of Monopoly the banker's role is to be a servant to all the players.   The banker's primary function is to distribute money to all the players and facilitate trade between them.   The one who plays the role of the banker does so without any special reward though they are usually chosen by agreement amongst all the players in consideration of that person's capability, honesty and integrity.

In the game there are two cardinal rules for the operation of the bank. Firstly; the banker can never run out of money. In fact, if necessary, the banker can create valid new currency on blank paper and issue as much additional currency as needed.   Secondly and

11

more importantly; the banker cannot issue money to himself and use it to play against the other players. The bank cannot become a player! This restriction makes great sense because for anyone to play with an unlimited supply of money would spell the ultimate ruin of everyone, other than the banker and any chosen accomplices.

The situation we find ourselves in now is that the bankers, in real life, are operating in the business world with relatively unlimited money. Consequently, bankers have developed coercive power over industry, education, politicians and the media. Bankers use the money they create to keep their privileged position as bankers relatively secure, whilst they work remorselessly to make their position totally unassailable.

As a means of centralizing power, the trading banks' system is unsurpassed and enterprisingly brilliant. The trading banks create and issue all new money by authorising new bank deposits. The new deposits are nearly always created in exchange for interest bearing debt obligations, which are repayable to the banks. The money creating process used within the trading bank system confers enormous power with minimal responsibility on those who work the magic of the money trick.

The purpose of this book is to expose the 'money trick' itself and more importantly, to reveal more equitable and democratic ways to issue and control money, than the destructive trading bank system.

The issue and control of money by private corporations has created unnecessary debt, to which most are now subservient and enslaved. This has placed a heavy yoke upon people, which must be lifted if mankind wants to act rationally and responsibly towards living standards and a sustainable environment.

The trading bank system automatically creates inflation and increasing debt, which are used to justify austerity measures, such as higher taxation and reduced social services but these provoke social unrest. The social unrest then justifies the development of police state powers, which allow the use of force to control the masses of indebted and dispossessed peoples.

2. Money is what money does.

What is money supposed to do?

The primary functions of money are to be: a medium of exchange; a unit of accounting and a store of value. However systemic inflation undermines the "store of value" function of money.

Historically money consisted of commodities that had a relatively high intrinsic (commodity) value, such as: salt, rum, copper, silver and gold. When such commodity money was placed (deposited) with someone else for safe storage, a receipt proving the deposit would be issued to the depositor. The receipt enabled the holder to reclaim the deposited goods or their equivalent. The receipt itself had no intrinsic value; it was just a paper receipt; a record of deposit; a deposit note. However, using these deposit notes as money greatly simplified trade. Debts could be settled using deposit notes and all such transactions bypassed the limitations of barter. The deposit notes had become money.

Gold and silver were universally accepted as money in trade. Thus, deposit notes issued for gold were, as one would often say, 'as good as gold' and the same applied to silver backed notes. The community knew from experience that they could exchange their deposit notes for gold whenever they wanted to, i.e. on demand.

Bank issued deposit notes, i.e. banknotes, functioned as money even better it would seem, than gold and silver. People had faith that they could exchange the notes for gold anytime they wanted but why would they bother? Their money was safer in the bank.

In an honest system, the gold or silver on deposit was exactly equal to the issued receipts, deposit notes. However, because there were no external checks and balances on the issue of commodity backed deposit notes, it was impossible for outsiders to know when additional notes were issued, even though no additional gold or silver had been placed on deposit. The bankers were then able to use duplicated (unbacked) deposit notes to make loans to other customers and to purchase all sorts of goods and services for themselves, whilst the public were none the wiser.

Long ago bankers realised that so long as they could keep the lid on the scam they would be receiving interest payments forever on credit created at the cost of a book entry. Secrecy became essential, to conceal and never reveal the deception.

What blurred matters further was the fact that people who'd received some payment in deposit notes would re-deposit the notes with the bank in return for a less negotiable record of deposit; a bank book for example. This added plausibility to the bankers' claim that any loans they made were other peoples' money which they were investing on behalf of the depositors.

Since the abandonment of the Gold Standard early last century no gold or silver is on deposit to back up the bank notes. Now one can only exchange bank notes for other bank notes or transfer the deposit to another account.

The truth of the present situation is that new money enters circulation whenever trading banks purchase anything; buildings, land, companies, computer systems, contractors, staff, bonus payments, anything that money can buy. Trading banks can purchase goods and services for themselves that they pay for with bank notes and bank cheques that they issue and honour themselves.

Being astute investors, bankers usually buy assets. The most common asset they buy is a promissory note issued by someone who wants to borrow money. What they actually borrow is bank credit. The borrower's promissory note is simply a loan application promising to deliver money to the bank at some rate over some period of time. It is an elaborate I.O.U. The bank's payment is made by simply creating a credit in the borrowers account.

The bank, just as likely, would further protect itself by obtaining a lien, a mortgage over real assets or someone else's personal guarantee, which bolster the value of the borrowers' promise to pay.

The new money created by this process enters circulation as a cost, to the borrower. Borrowers must eventually recoup the cost of this money through the prices they charge for their goods and services or face foreclosure and bankruptcy.

Thus any expansion in the money supply under this system will cause general prices to rise by the amount of new money created. So inflation is systemic in the current banking system.

Whilst in the past all sorts of objects have been used as money; now nearly all trade is done with money that has no physical existence at all and is backed up with nothing. Money only works because we have faith and confidence in it.

Money has no intrinsic value unless the money is in a physically valuable form such as gold and silver coins.

Money actually enables claims to be made on existing goods and services which are "real wealth". When there is no real wealth available, money has little if any value. For example, in a situation of having a million dollars, even in cash, but when lost in a desert, with no water, food, shelter or means of communication, one would quickly realise money is only a potential claim on the real wealth of others. A claim that is only valid if others are willing to part with their real wealth in exchange for the money.

Money can only function as a medium of exchange when the seller believes in it, no matter what "it" is. Belief is essential. The word "Credit" can be traced back to the Latin "Credo", which means "I believe". We can see this same root word used in other words like "credibility" and "credence", words that carry the idea of belief.

Under normal circumstances we obtain our needs and serve each other through an exchange of goods and services. Money facilitates this mutually beneficial exchange in a market where the seller parts with real wealth in exchange for money tickets, which are simply tokens. The seller is not overly concerned with the type of payment, so long as a valid deposit results after processing by their bank. It is immaterial whether the deposit takes the form of notes, coins, cheques, credit card vouchers or electronic funds transfer.

Money functions as a form of inducement that is used by others to induce us to work for them and to get others to work for us. Most people would willingly part with almost all of their possessions and most of their time, if they were offered enough inducement. Money, being a relatively peaceful form of inducement is preferable to brute force. Money also functions as a sort of universal, undated, claim ticket, within the economy in which it was issued and of course without money there is almost no access to goods and services in that economy.

Modern money can therefore be better understood when considered as a privately issued ticketing system, which has substantially become electronic. We trade goods and services in the market by using this electronic ticketing system. When we trade with one another, unless we use cash or a loan account, the financial component of the trade consists of an adjustment to the record of deposits in the banking system. Thus one can come to the realisation that deposits in the banking system are money even though bank deposits have no physical existence.

Incidentally, only "current" bank deposits can be drawn down (spent) at any time, either by transfer to another account or withdrawn in cash as currency. Currency describes any and all notes and coins in the hands of the public. Currency is the small change of the money system.

Current deposits and notes and coins are obviously interchangeable. "Term" deposits on the other hand are generally not available till they mature.

Money loses much of its persuasive power over people when people feel they already have enough money. The perception as to when we have enough money is a matter of attitude. Many would consider themselves desperately short of money when they have what others would consider, great wealth. When we have enough money we willingly part with some of it in exchange for the things we need or want.

Common problems associated with money.

- Debt: In practice the major down side of money for most people is debt. People and nations with serious money problems usually have a debt problem.

- Inflation: Money almost continuously loses its purchasing power, which is called "inflation". Inflation is a form of theft. We'll come to that later.

- Artificial scarcity. Artificial scarcity results in money being treated as a commodity; yet it is in fact an abstract and virtually costless unit of accounting. How can money, have a price, in money? Only because of artificial scarcity.

The crux of the money and debt problems is that our nation's money supply is privately issued, for profit, by commercial bankers. Enormous power is in the hands of whoever controls the terms and condition under which new money is created and issued.

Mayer Amschel Rothschild, a prominent European banker in the eighteenth century is reported to have said, "Permit me to issue and control the money of the nation and I care not who makes its laws." — This quote will be analysed in more detail shortly.

For the moment, it is worth noting that the underlying motive of the bankers, who issue all money, cannot be to "make money", in the normal sense of the word, because they control the source of all money. Their only logical motive then is to further their corporate interests and agenda.

Unfortunately the deception inherent in the present financial system has apparently deceived and corrupted those supposedly controlling it. The financial manipulation inherent in the trading bank system provides near unlimited, hidden and hence irresponsible power. Irresponsible power facilitates corrupt and psychopathic behaviour. They care no more about the destruction of people and even nations, than the death of a sparrow.

Commercial Trading Banks are man-made, soulless, amoral, corporate entities that were birthed in deception. They are historically destructive and psychopathic in their behaviour despite concocted appearances of honesty, security and morality.

It is little wonder that Yeshua the Messiah (Jesus the Christ) said "You cannot serve God and money". (Matthew 6:24 ESV)

The "money supply", also called "money stock", in an economy is the summed face value of all notes and coins in the hands of the public, plus deposits in the banking system. The amount on deposit in the banking system far exceeds the value of notes and coins. Certainly, in Australia, this is the case. Bank deposits exceed the value of notes and coins by about twenty-six to one.

In Australia, "M3" is the economic symbol used to indicate the sum total of notes plus coins plus deposits in savings and trading banks. *(The Reserve Bank of Australia Glossary.* www.rba.gov.au/glossary/index.html)

When deposits in Non-Bank Financial Institutions (NBFI) such as credit unions and building societies are included the total is called *Broad Money*. However to avoid unnecessary complexity we will leave the aggregate figures of broad money aside for the moment. Credit issued by Commercial Trading Banks, creates new deposits. Deposits in the banking system are, by definition, money.

Incidentally, the operation of so called "Sharia Banking" (Islamic) is almost identical and offers no hope to solve the central problem; the monopolistic ownership and control of money as it is created.

"Fractional-reserve banking is the most common form of banking and is practiced in almost all countries. Although Islamic banking prohibits the making of profit from interest on debt, a form of fractional-reserve banking is still evident in most Islamic countries." *(Wikipedia)*.

In Australia and the USA, "State Government Banks" offer a practical starting point to address the real problem. Within its own state, a state government bank can issue and distribute money; as bank cheques and credit transfers to other bank accounts.

Please note: a State bank doesn't need deposits before creating additional money. Banks are the source of all money. Bank purchases are the original source of all deposited funds. Trading bank purchases create deposits, not the other way around.

The constitution of any new State Bank must prevent the bank from owing the money it creates or supplying new money direct to State government to be spent as it, (the government), sees fit.

The distribution of state bank issued credit, other than that used to finance local consumer subsidies, must be done equally to the individual citizens of the State. It is for the citizens to spend or invest the new credit as they see fit. Regular payments should to be made equally to all adult citizens and must be free of interest, debt and tax. Such payments should be in addition to all other sources of income.

This policy is the exact opposite policy to what the "Banksters" have traditionally wanted; which is "endless interest bearing debt", "no subsidies" and "progressive taxation".

The practice of so called fractional reserve banking is really a story the bankers dreamed up to legitimize their creation of money out of nothing.

In future banks will be allowed to store your money or lend your money but not both at the same time.

The simplest way to eliminate the dishonesty of fractional reserve banking is to progressively raise the fractional reserve ratio requirement.

"The reserve requirement (cash reserve ratio) is a central bank regulation that sets the minimum reserves each commercial bank must hold of customer deposits and notes." *(Wikipedia).*

When the fractional reserve reaches 100% banks will be unable to create any new money.

The economic effect of raising the fractional reserve ratio is that the existing money supply will start to contract. The contraction is because bank debts can only be repaid with existing deposits. Just as bank loans create both new debt and new deposits, so when the transaction goes the other way a deposit must be used to repay bank debt. Both the debt and the deposit used to pay the debt cease to exist.

Without a corresponding issue of new money existing deposits must be used to repay bank debt. This causes a contraction in the money supply and is usually economically undesirable. A contraction in the money supply is how banks create recessions and depressions. They call in existing loans and decline or raise the price of new ones.

It is worth repeating that a simple and undeniably fair way to maintain a stable money supply (money stock) whilst at the same time paying down existing debts will be by the issue of replacement money at the same rate as the repayment of bank debt. This process will avert any contraction in the economy whilst bank debt is eliminated.

It is worth remembering that **bank debt starts out as a record of the amount of credit created**.

Usury (charging interest) at the point of issue is absurd and indefensible. However this situation will be fully remedied when the fractional reserve ratio reaches 100% and the current banks are no longer in a position to issue new money and claim the ownership and distribution rights of it all for themselves.

The upside of this is that bankers will become what many bank staff already believe they are; valued servants of the community and not in any way fearful masters and so called 'Banksters'.

Probably very few trading bank managers realize they create money "out of nothing" when they issue bank credit. They think they lend their depositors' funds; i.e. the deposits in their bank. But point out to them that depositor's funds don't decrease when loans are made; and also that new loans will result in new deposits somewhere else in the system. Then ask them where the resulting increases in total deposits comes from; and they might just start to catch on.

The proposals in this book, when implemented, will be somewhat like bringing fire under control. I say this thinking of the old adage; fire can be a wonderful servant but a fearful master.

Democratically distributed State, National or other social credit can be used to reduce and eliminate total debt in an equitable way without relying on foreign sources of funding. Issuing social credit dividend payments to all citizens and implementing an efficiency subsidy on local products are two policy mechanisms that have the potential to redress the money problems listed earlier, namely: Debt, inflation and artificial scarcity.

Even after having paid back and extinguished the national debt it will be necessary to continue to issue money to all citizens, so as to create and maintain a balance between the available real wealth in the market and the money supply available to consumers.

A predictable result of the implementation of these proposals is that the production system in any State can be expected to rebound, due to a surge in demand. There may well be a preference by citizens, who are no longer artificially short of money, to purchase quality local products and invest in local businesses. Local, relatively cashed up consumers will place a steady demand on local production; stimulate local employment and promote self-sufficiency.

Given that money is mostly intangible, yet it motivates the minds of men, perhaps the idea of money came from a non-physical source, i.e. spiritual. If that is the case it seems reasonable to me that mankind's historic spiritual adversary, Satan, could have inspired the debt and usury based financial system. Perhaps this was what Satan had in mind when, over two thousand years ago, he offered to Yeshua (Jesus) the Son of Elohim, King of Isra'el, all the kingdoms of the world, if Yeshua would bow down and worship him, (just once). That offer was totally rejected by the Messiah. This is recorded in the Bible's book of Matthew 4:8-10 " [8]Once more, the Adversary took him up to the summit of a very high mountain, showed him all the kingdoms of the world in all their glory, [9] and said to him, "All this I will give you if you will bow down and worship me." [10]"Away with you, Satan!" Yeshua (Jesus) told him, "For the Tanakh (Old Testament) says, 'Worship Y'HoVaH (God of Israel) your Elohim (God), and serve only him.'""

The same offer was obviously accepted by others of lower rank than He who was executed as the King of the Jews; as well as by other people, both before and since. The system progressively tempts people into becoming devoted to money. Devotion is akin to worship.

The system that Satan may have invented has a natural consequence of war and environmental destruction. For example; the military industrial complex has grown because it doesn't have to sell its products to the ultimate consumers. Its products are given away, whether the consumers want them or not. The hapless consumers receive bombs, bullets and missiles, all of which are destroyed on impact, which as a matter of course necessitates the production of replacement products.

The problem of environmental destruction, which the debt and usury based, banking system causes, is used as an excuse to justify a policy of population reduction on a massive scale, called Eugenics. As I see it, Satan's goal is to have mankind worship and serve him and he'll use his servants to eliminate anyone who won't. Satan hates humans; they undoubtedly remind him of his Creator and the Messiah who has and will defeat him. Satan doesn't even like this planet, after all he was cast out of heaven down to here, so it is his prison; his Prison Planet.

The progressive centralisation of financial power that can be witnessed worldwide is ongoing and dates back over several millennia. For a detailed historical account of this, you can read David Astle's book *The Babylonian Woe*, which is freely available online at the following website.

www.archive.org/details/TheBabylonianWoe

3. Forms of Money.

Money can, and has taken many forms in its history. Metals, shells, beads, animal and fish teeth, salt, rum, playing cards, notched sticks, etc. The list is almost boundless.

In the modern economy Currency is deemed to be; metal coins and folding paper and or plastic notes.

Currency.

The Reserve Bank of Australia (RBA) uses the following definition of currency.

"'Currency' comprises holdings of notes and coins by the private non-bank sector."

Notice the location. Currency only exists in the private NON-Bank sector. Therefore notes and coins, when in the bank, aren't classed as currency. Currency may be considered as money in any "tangible" form "when in actual use" as a medium of exchange, most commonly as circulating paper notes and coins. Bank deposits, on the other hand, are intangible. They have no physical existence what so ever, they are just an entry in a bank account. Regardless of money being tangible or intangible, money is of very little immediate use if the goods and services desired are not available and for sale.

Precious Metal Currency.

Barter is trading without money. Valuable metals like copper, silver and gold have been used as convenient and divisible items of barter. When precious metals are minted into coins and used as currency it is akin to barter. The nominal value of coins must equal or exceed the bullion value or such coins will just as likely be melted back to bullion. When the nominal value of coins exceeds the bullion value, the coins are, by definition, fiat currency.)

Large copper Australian pennies began disappearing from circulation as inflation caused the bullion price to exceed the face value.

Australian silver coins were finally abandoned in 1967 for the same reason. Conversion to decimal currency began on the 14th of February 1966. The last Australian silver coin was the first Australian 50 cent piece. It was round and made from 80% silver and 20% copper. It was much like the extremely popular 1964 United States John F. Kennedy Silver Half-Dollar. The total silver content of the Australian silver 50 cent coin was 0.3416 oz. "Subsequent changes in the prevailing silver price … meant ultimately that it was a single year issue with the decision to no longer release them made in July 1967. It was replaced by a 12 sided (dodecagonal) copper-nickel issue.

Source: www.cruzis-coins.com/50c/

The following images dramatically show the impact of inflation on purchasing power. In 1966 the fifty cent coin cost fifty cents. How many fifty cent coins do you think it would take to purchase that same coin now?

Figure 1. 80% silver 1966 Australian fifty cent coin.

The April 2012 price of silver was about AUD$31.50 per oz. Now it takes twenty-four 2012 fifty cent coins to buy one 1966 silver fifty cent coin. The silver hasn't changed, monetary inflation devalued the currency.

Figure 2. The twenty-four fifty cent coins above have a similar value to the silver in one 1966 fifty cent coin.

Gold becomes currency when it is cast into coins and is impressed with a common number and a stamp of authority. Gold was a commodity minted into currency for centuries. Traders show interest in the inscription on coins to increase their faith that the metal is pure and the weight correct. The relative scarcity of gold will cause problems if trade is limited to its availability.

Gold is potentially an aesthetically useful metal. It is comparatively easy to work into objects of art and great beauty. Gold has some utility value; it is very stable and does not tarnish. As a common item of barter gold facilitated trade and is readily divisible into smaller units whilst maintaining a stable weight for value ratio as bullion.

However gold coins are too soft to be of practical use as coins in an industrial society. A gold annual demand chart on www.kitco.com shows that demand has fallen since the peak around the turn of this century. Their annual Gold Demand chart shows the main use of gold is for: jewellery ~58 million ounces; electronics ~6 million oz.; dentistry ~2 million oz. and all other uses about 5 million oz.

If gold were not idolised and horded in stockpiles, there is probably no real shortage for the practical uses of gold. Idolising and hoarding gold may also be artificially propping up (manipulating) the price.

The idea is sometimes presented that we should use gold as a reserve for all money and return to a sort of gold standard. However it would be foolish for any modern economy to artificially restrict trading activity to the happenstance availability of some metal of limited productive value.

Fiat Currency.

Fiat currency refers to any tokens that are declared by an authority to be legal tender in its area of jurisdiction. Very much the same as gaming chips are in a casino. Legal tender can be used for payments of all financial debts and the creditor must accept.

Logically as an economy grows more money is needed. In fact it would be more accurate to say that historically more money enables an economy to grow until limited by either physical or consumption constraints.

Fiat currency is sometimes criticised with the false claim that fiat money always looses value through inflation. However inflation can be created or stopped by changing how money enters circulation. Whenever fiat currency looses value it does so as a result of policies imposed by those who can control the issue of money and how it is put into circulation.

Given that currency is only around 5% of the total money supply it is absurd to blame inflation on fiat currency.

Bank Deposits.

All bank deposits in Australia are, by definition, money. This money is has no physical existence and only exists as a record in the various ADI - Authorized deposit-taking institution. ADIs (banks, building societies and credit unions) are supervised by the Australian Prudential Regulation Authority (APRA).

Transferring bank deposits from one account to another is a very efficient way to quickly move purchasing power (money) throughout the community without the need to move physical currency.

The Reserve Bank of Australia (RBA) uses quite practical distinctions between the differ types of money that make up the money supply in Australia. When they groups different types of money together they call the mix, an aggregate.

The Reserve Bank of Australia Glossary.

www.rba.gov.au/glossary/index.html

Monetary Aggregates consist of:

'M1' defined as currency plus bank current deposits of the private non-bank sector;

'M3' defined as **M1 plus all other bank deposits** of the private non-bank sector;

'Broad money' defined as M3 plus borrowings from the private sector by NBFIs, less the latter's holdings of currency and bank deposits;

'Money base' defined as holdings of banknotes and coins by the private sector plus deposits of banks with the Reserve Bank of Australia (RBA) and other RBA liabilities to the private non-bank sector.

Current Bank Deposits (At Call).

Current bank deposits, which are "at call" are classified with currency, just like notes and coins in the M1 grouping of monetary aggregates. Current deposits are referred to as, "at call", because these funds may be called upon by depositors anytime and withdrawn as cash by the public. Note that cash in private non-bank sector, (i.e. in the hands of the public) is part of M1 but cash in the banks is not included.

Current bank deposits come into existence from either; currency deposits or transfers from other accounts like loan accounts, maturing fixed term deposits and various bank purchases.

Fixed term deposits.

Fixed term deposits can't be accessed until the end of some designated time. This is the apparent reason that the RBA (Reserve Bank of Australia) excludes term deposits from what they call M1.

NIFI (Non-Bank Financial Institution) Deposits.

The deposits in non-bank financial institutions like CUBS (Credit Unions and Building Societies), finance companies and the like are not included in the M3 money aggregate.

When NIFI deposits are added to the M3 aggregate the total is called "Broad Money".

Unlike trading banks, the non-bank financial institutions actually do lend from the pool of money deposited with them. If one makes some specific enquiries it will be revealed that they too are bank customers. These non-trading bank financial institutions deposit the funds they receive with some bank and make loans by writing cheques on, or withdrawing funds from, their pooled deposit account at their bank.

Their deposit at the bank is reduced by the amount of any loan they make; thus their loans do not increase the volume of money (M3) although they do increase the volume of what is called, in Australia, "Broad Money".

Non-bank financial institutions are vulnerable to trading bank imposed credit squeezes. During such times many of their customers may seek to withdraw their funds. The potentially risky trading position of these institutions is because their business structure is to "borrow short and lend long". If there is a run on their deposits they become insolvent. The infamous collapse of the Pyramid Building Society in Victoria in 1990 is a case in point. "Pyramid was Victoria's largest building society and Australia's second largest. The Victorian Government ultimately 'bailed out' depositors at a cost to taxpayers of over $900 million, leaving other creditors and investors, including holders of redeemable preference shares to bear losses." http://fsgstudy.treasury.gov.au/content/Davis_Report/04_Ch apter2.asp

When building societies and other non-trading bank financial institutions make loans there is no change to the volume of money (M3). This is because any money they lend already exists as currency or bank deposits. This is not the case with loans (credit) from trading banks.

Banks Purchases Create Deposits.

It is time to take a revealing look behind the facade of banking and see clearly the way credit and debt are created. I pray you see past the mental sleight of hand, the trick in the logic, which has brought us into progressive bondage. Families and children are sacrificed as individuals devote their lives attempting to serve and appease the demands imposed by the interest bearing debt that the banking system produces.

Given that **bank deposits are money** then it follows that any process that creates new bank deposits is a process that creates money. Because this is the case, creating money is surprisingly simple.

Money creation can be better understood with the following insights.

Every trading bank loan, purchase or interest payment creates new deposits and so expands the money supply. That is, unless the loan is used to pay an existing bank debt, in which case there is no change in the money supply. The reverse is also true. Whenever deposits are used for the repayment of trading bank loans or to purchase bank assets the money supply is reduced, because deposits are extinguished upon being returned to their source. Much like in JRR Tolkin's trilogy "The Lord of the Rings", where the power of the "one ring" is destroyed when returned to Mount Doom and cast into the fiery volcanic pit of hell from which it was created.

When a borrower completes and signs a loan application they create a promissory note in which the applicant promises to pay certain sums into the future to the note holder. The promissory note is an obvious asset and the bank may decide to purchase and pay for it. Whenever banks purchase assets they pay for them by creating new current deposits. Current deposits are by definition, money and the increase in total deposits made by bank purchases becomes additional money in circulation.

Interest payments to their depositors are also a form of bank purchase. They are paying to have funds deposited with them. Is it not indeed strange that trading banks pay for deposits that they record only as liabilities? Paying for liabilities in this way is part for the smoke screen around the deception.

We are now in a position to understand that the entire money supply has come into existence only because banks purchase assets, which they pay for with book entries. Bankers are in the fortunate position of being able to purchase whatever they like at no real cost to themselves by creating money, the means of payment, out of nothing.

The entities called trading banks have gained irresponsible power over the community through banking licences we unwittingly granted them.

Lord Acton famously revealed that an accumulation of irresponsible power produces corruption, both in the power structure itself and within the community over which such power is irresponsibly exercised. Irresponsible power corrupts the systems of society: law, media, education, language, the lot.

There is a fundamental deception causing the legion of ills that plague the civilised world. As a result of this deception, unredeemable debt has become a seemingly insurmountable problem. I believe unredeemable debt is a satanic method of bondage.

The economy is operating in what amount to a generally unrealized deception in the accounting procedures of banking. Long ago truth was dismissed. Now, though perhaps with the best of intentions, we unwittingly attempt to conduct honest business within an economy ruled by a corrupted financial system.

THE LIGHT YOKE

The effective policy of the private banking system is for there to be an artificial scarcity of money unless it is serving their ends. This policy creates a money problem at almost all levels of society. The policy disrupts and compromises the very interface of trade and relationships. The phenomenon of increasing unredeemable national and world debt is a manifestation of the deliberatively deceptive design of the trading bank system and the policy of its controllers and inventor.

The Money Changers (Debt Merchants).

Proverbs 22:7 The rich rules over the poor, and the borrower is servant to the lender. (NKJ).

As a community we need to trade with one another and so the provision of money is virtually essential for any significant endeavour by a community. Money facilitates trade and so no major human endeavour, be it for good or ill is possible without the provision of money. We have become dependent on money, yet it is a man-made abstraction.

Throughout the world, the standard financial procedure is to issue virtually all new money in exchange for interest bearing debt obligations. This practice makes it a mathematical certainty that total debt will progressively exceed issued credit. The staggering proportions of world debt need not be surprising, they are mathematically inevitable; and planned to be that way.

It is interesting to note that every nation on earth is in the same position with regard to massive financial debt. The debt of the U.S.A. is several trillions of dollars and even Japan with a huge trading surplus still has a gigantic internal debt, of a similar, unimaginable magnitude.

Nations don't owe money to other nations; they owe money to international book keeping organizations called banks.

There is no mechanism within the world's financial system to redeem total debt. Bank debts may be and are written off at the whim of the banks. Other debts may be rolled into new loans often with new conditions. During times of general credit expansion the terms may be easier but all too often this is not the case and austerity may be imposed upon the hapless borrowers, be they nations or individuals. Even Bankruptcy and the transfer to the bankers of title deeds to real wealth are only temporary. On an international level such transfers are called "debt for equity swaps".

Trading bank licences bestow the legal right to create new money and use it to purchase debt obligations (promissory notes). The fact that new bank credit is offered as loans is ample proof of the claim of ownership of all the new money the banks create and issue as credit.

All bank credit functions as money in that it confers a right to claim goods and services from the community's open market and can be used to cancel debt. Obviously to claim ownership of all new money is effectively the same as claiming the ownership of nearly all the communities' goods and services. By owning and controlling the issue of new credit the banks, which physically are non-productive organisations, exercise unmerited, irresponsible power and control over the economic life and activity of the whole community.

Obviously money has no value in an empty market, so money only has value if the economy of that currency has available real wealth, which sellers are prepared to exchange for the currency. The implicit belief of the seller is that they can use the currency to either reduce their debt or exchange the money for other real wealth, (goods and services).

Trading bank loans produce an increase in the total volume of money (M3). The loan creates new current deposits whilst no existing bank deposit is diminished. When they lend cash, this cash also becomes extra currency in circulation. Remember cash in a bank is not currency because it is "out of circulation".

New credit is issued by the bank and the borrower's promise to repay the debt is written into the books, as an asset. This helps explain why banks don't like early repayments, because early repayments reduce their assets.

The process of rolling over loans or re-scheduling loans is simply the issue of a new loan to pay the principal of an existing loan. The volume of money (M3) is unchanged if the amounts are the same.

The only way to cancel a debt is with a credit. If the credit is issued as a loan it cannot cancel debt, it can only roll the debt onto someone else.

It is in attempting to conduct business against a background of rising and inextinguishable financial debt that individuals and nations find themselves fighting economic warfare and ultimately military warfare against their economic rivals. Debt and the risk of insolvency are the artificially imposed financial incentives that cause the ongoing destruction of societies and the natural environment of the planet.

Answers.com has the primary meaning of the word "worship" as: "The reverent love and devotion accorded a deity, an idol, or a sacred object." The expression "almighty dollar" is not new and devotion is akin to worship. Most of mankind is currently deceived into worship and service of an un-Godly manmade abstraction called money. Serving one another through a debt based money system automatically transitions into wage slavery. The addition of usury makes the debt unredeemable and so mankind is in danger of being totally enslaved to the service of Mammon, serving the demonically inspired, man-made and false idol of this world - money.

Consider this quote by Yeshua HaMashiyach (Jesus the Christ) in the Biblical book of Matthew.

Matthew 6:24 "No one can serve two masters. Either he will hate the one and love the other, or he will be devoted to the one and despise the other. You cannot serve both God and Money." (NIV). Other Bible versions use Mammon in place of Money.

A logical conclusion from this quote is that those who love money will hate those who love the one and only Almighty Creator, Our Heavenly Father, YHVH.

Amschel Mayer Rothschild (1773-1855), in 1838 said: "Permit me to issue and control the money of a nation, and I care not who makes its laws."

His statement carries with it serious implication, such as that those individuals who control and issue the money supply consider themselves effectively above the law. Also, the right to issue and control money confers effective ownership of the money supply.

Rothschild's statement also reveals likely banker priorities in circumstances where they are not permitted to issue and control the money of a nation. Under these circumstances, all they care about is how to change the laws to enable them to issue and control the money of that nation. Sovereign rulers make laws, so an obvious tactic would be to finance a revolution and replace the ruler. Control of the media is essential, so a current practice is to finance and thus make willing servants of media moguls who will buy up independent media outlets. In representative democracies they need to control the political representatives. The easy way to do this is to finance and so control political parties that choose and control politicians. The goal being, by any means, fair or foul, to change the laws so that Rothschild and associates issue and control the money of all nations.

For a banker to be effectively above the law they had to both issue *and* control the money. However the issuance (creation) of money and its control, which together are like ownership need not necessarily be linked. This is especially the case when what is created has no physical existence and is almost costless to produce. The issue or creation of money actually occurs as a bank deposit is recorded and also but to a much lesser extent, when currency is carried from a bank.

We all know that an uncleared cheque is not yet money. Much as a ballot paper is not a vote until it is cast.

At this point it is worth considering the role of a government electoral commission. The Electoral Commission creates all the new votes needed for each election and referendum. Obviously the commission doesn't own all the votes, nor select who amongst the citizens gets to vote and for that matter, how many votes they get. No, all the new votes produced by the commission are shared out equally amongst all the eligible citizens.

If the Electoral Commissioner could issue and control all the votes then the whole electoral process would be corrupted and the results disastrous. In the same way, when private commercial trading banks issue and control the money supply of a nation then the economy (money system) is inevitably corrupted and the results disastrous.

The democratic and decentralising principle we are so familiar with when we freely receive our ballot papers from the Electoral Commission can also be applied to the creation and distribution of all new money. Then financial corruption, which is inevitable in a system based on deceit, will cease to be inherent part of the economic system.

A license, by definition, is a permit to do something illegal. Historically, those permitted (licensed) to create money do so for personal profit, power and influence. They have used every means that money can buy to extend and maintain the benefits from such licences. The power conferred by a license to create money is enormous and predictably corrupting. It seems some individuals would rather see the world substantially reduced to ashes then yield up their immoral claims to the ownership and control of all newly created money.

4. Creating New Money Disguised.

The trading bank system creates virtually all money in the form of new deposits, which are created by bank purchases. Bank purchases are mostly of promissory notes, which in effect issues new money into circulation in exchange for interest bearing debt obligations owed to the bank.

Every loan by a commercial trading bank is recorded in their books as an asset. However they undertake no corresponding liability.

A look at the major items on the balance sheet of trading banks show "loans out" as the largest asset; whilst a similar item on the liability side of their balance sheet is "deposits". There is an apparent balance but it is a false balance.

Proverbs 11:1 A false balance is abomination to the LORD... (KJV)

The Commonwealth Bank of Australia used to be a government owned trading bank. The table below was excerpted from a USA Disclosure Document published on line by the bank. The table demonstrates the fact point that commercial trading banks don't declare the asset value of their deposits.

The following link was to the source document.

http://www.commbank.com.au/about-us/shareholders/us-investors/docs/U.S_Disclosure_Document_240910.pdf

Commonwealth Bank of Australia Annual U.S. Disclosure Document 2010 Page 14

Consolidated Balance Sheet Data

Assets ($M)	2010	2009
Loans, advances and other receivables	**418,453**	**493,459**
Total Assets	**548,088**	**646,330**
Liabilities ($M)		
Deposits and other public borrowings	**317,714**	**374,663**
Total Liabilities	**506,465**	**597,247**

These amounts show that in 2010 that bank loans, advances and other receivables are 76% of their total assets.

The figures also show that deposits and other public borrowings are 62% of total liabilities.

Notice that there is no mention of the asset value of deposits and borrowed funds. Deposits are money held in trust for customers. The Reserve Bank of Australia (RBA) classes deposits as part of the M3 money supply. The amount on deposit is not reduced by the banks making loans. On the contrary loans create more deposits, either immediately or when the new bank credit is spent into circulation.

The following table shows how the data can also be presented to substantiate the myth that trading banks lend deposits (borrowed money) and profit from the margin between the two. Note all amounts are in millions of dollars.

Page 8 Commonwealth Bank of Australia Annual U.S. Disclosure Document 2010

As at	30/06/10	30/06/09
Average interest earning assets. ($M)	553,735	385,667
Average interest bearing liabilities ($M)	521,338	362,249
Net interest margin (%)	2.13%	2.10%

Is it valid for banks to record deposited funds only as a liability? Are they not also an asset?

Every other business and individual for that matter, upon receiving money to hold in trust for someone (a deposit) would record it as both an asset and a liability. So it will appear in a balance sheet on both sides of the account of assets and liabilities. The deposit must appear as both an asset and as a liability; an asset because they hold the funds and also as a liability, because the funds were deposited in trust and have to be paid back.

The peculiar thing about **commercial trading banks is they don't record the asset value of funds deposited with them.** Deposited funds are only shown as a liability. Thus, in effect, declaring that bank issued credit has no value in such a bank. In a sense this is quite true, for the new deposit may be no more than the presentation of the banks own cheques drawn on a loan accounts they had earlier created.

Generally the closer one gets to the source of a commercial product the lower the price. The lowest just or fair price is the cost of production. Now, the physical "cost of production" of a commercial bank loan is a "book entry". Thus perhaps they can reason that deposited credit, which functions as money for everyone else, has no value "in" a commercial trading bank because they can create such deposits at will.

All other financial institutions must include funds deposited with them as assets (and liabilities). So their assets include their loans to others (trade debtors), their plant and equipment plus their financial assets, including deposits (loans) from others.

Commercial trading banks only record their depositor's funds as bank liabilities and in so doing successfully hide, conceal and never reveal an otherwise obvious truth that **trading banks never lend their deposits.**

Instead of lending their deposits commercial trading banks create loan accounts, which are listed in their books as assets to balance the book liability of their deposits. The whole process creates the appearance of honestly balanced books. By this simple trick, commercial banks hide their creation of bank credit out of nothing. The credit they issue in turn creates more deposits and the cycle continues. The commercial banks then receive perpetual interest payments till the loan is repaid. Loans are issued to whoever the banks choose. Loans may be arbitrarily forgiven or recalled. If a recalled loan is not paid on demand, debtors may be pursued to bankruptcy and confiscation of the debtors' assets. All of which is conducted legally, although of questionable morality, in accordance with the policy of the trading banks own agenda.

Presumably the top item on the (hidden) agenda of the commercial trading banks is the preservation of the permit to issue and control the nation's money supply, in accordance with the Rothschild quote mentioned earlier.

For these commercial banks, the only liabilities associated with deposited funds are to maintain the confidence of their customers and to facilitate the transfer of deposits between accounts for customers. There is apparently no actual liability. Commercial trading banks also seem to have control over the distribution of all new fiat currency; the printed notes and minted coins of legal tender.

When new money (bank credit) is issued, through the process of asset (promissory note) purchase, title deeds to real property are usually mortgaged as security for the bank. At this point two things should be noted. Firstly, the bank claims the ownership of the new credit though it parted with nothing to create it; and secondly; the numerical size of the debt will be progressively increased by compound interest.

The banking industry is not actively involved in the physical production process. When a bank makes a loan it does not physically or actually part with anything. As well as this, when the trading banks issue credit they write the borrower's repayment pledge into their books as an asset and hold a lien over the real wealth offered as security.

Commercial trading banks can be obscenely lucrative because their trading bank licenses allow them to create money for asset purchases at no real cost to themselves. Banking licences may allow for bank activity to be reined in but when unconstrained, the licences bestow upon banks almost unlimited power over society.

The nation's money supply is created by data entries in bank computers, is in effect rented by the community. The community should own and control the source of its money. If it did it would be possible to issue sufficient money to enable all the citizens to purchase their share of that rapidly increasing proportion of national production that is not represented by wages, salaries and dividends.

Money is created when commercial banks purchase securities, promissory notes and other assets. Commercial banks pay for these assets by making credit entries of virtual deposits into the sellers' bank accounts. The new deposits expand the money supply because bank deposits are, by definition, money.

Banks demand that all borrowers; individuals, corporations and governments honour the terms and conditions of their loan agreements. Failure to do so may result in banks foreclosing on any real wealth the borrowers own.

We need to remember the Biblical proverb:

Proverbs 22:7 The rich rules over the poor, and the borrower {is} servant to the lender.

Communities and nations are being herded into bondage to mammon because of a devilishly deceptive financial system. Accepting commercial bank credit as a valid addition to the money supply leads to social indebtedness.

The Myth of Fractional Reserve Banking.

"Savers looking to keep their valuables in safekeeping depositories deposited gold coins and silver coins at goldsmiths, receiving in turn a note for their deposit. Once these notes became a trusted medium of exchange an early form of paper money was born, in the form of the goldsmiths' notes.

"As the notes were used directly in trade, the goldsmiths observed that people would not usually redeem all their notes at the same time."

Source: www.thefreedictionary.com *Fractional-reserve banking*

They observed that only about 10% of the deposited gold was ever withdrawn as gold. So in their own interests a reserve requirement of around 10% was found to be sufficient to cover normal demand for actual gold. This created a dishonest opportunity: the goldsmiths could with relatively safety, quietly issue nine times their total deposited gold stock as duplicate deposit receipts. They could lend these duplicated deposit notes at interest. The cost of the additional notes was negligible but they were now earning interest on money they created out of nothing.

There was a potential downside to the dishonest practice of issuing more receipts than deposited gold. "... However, if creditors, the note holders of gold originally deposited, lost confidence (faith) in the ability of a bank to redeem (pay) their notes (in gold), many would try to redeem their notes at the same time. If in response a bank could not raise enough funds by calling in loans or selling bills, it either went into insolvency or defaulted on its notes. Such a situation is called a "bank run" and caused the demise of many early banks."

(www.thefreedictionary.com *Fractional-reserve banking*)

These practices and the established ratios evolved into what is now known as the fractional reserve banking system.

In modern so called fractional reserve banking the idea is presented that deposits somehow provide a reserve to protect the bank from a run on its deposits. Yet as we saw earlier the commercial trading banks do not record their deposits as assets; only as liabilities. This being the case it begs the question; how is a liability supposed to somehow function as a reserve. Whilst using deposits as a reserve may have had some validity when deposits had some intrinsic value, this is no longer the case.

The myth continues with the banking practice of requiring a deposit from potential borrowers. Perhaps the deposit becomes the mythical fractional reserve, even though a deposit is a liability for the bank.

Modern Historical Origins

"The Bank hath benefit of interest on all monies, which it creates out of nothing." The boastful statement of William Patterson, the Financiers' 'Front Man' and co-founder of the (privately owned) Bank of England. Founded in 1694". www.cqfreestate.com/banking.html

In the English speaking world, Government sanctioned, fractional reserve banking started a little over three hundred years ago in 1694 with the establishment of the Bank of England. The government needed to raise money to fight a war against Louis XIV.

The following, quite revealing quotes are from the Bank of England's website.

www.bankofengland.co.uk/about/Pages/history/timeline.aspx#1

"The goldsmith bankers had been damaged … There were calls for a national or public bank to mobilise the nation's resources. Many schemes were proposed. The successful one, from William Paterson, envisaged a loan of £1,200,000 to the Government, in return for which the subscribers would be incorporated as the 'Governor and Company of the Bank of England'. The Royal Charter was sealed on 27 July 1694, and the Bank started its role as the Government's banker and debt-manager, which it continues today."

The Bank of England is privately owned!

"The Bank's early years were dominated by the Government's pressing demands for finance and the issue of a new coinage. The Bank also embarked upon a conventional banking business, accepting deposits and discounting bills. As evidence of deposits placed with it the Bank issued banknotes, initially in odd sums, with pounds, shilling and pence, but later in round amounts.

"The Bank's notes became a widely accepted currency; people seldom doubted that the "promise to pay" (which then referred to gold coin of the realm) would be honoured.

"The national debt increased steadily during the eighteenth century, from £12mn in 1700 to £850mn by the end of the Napoleonic wars. Those wars put great strain on the nation's finances and in 1797 the drain on the Bank's gold reserves made it necessary to stop paying out gold in exchange for the Bank's notes."

Australia's first trading bank, the Bank of New South Wales, was established in 1817 under a charter of incorporation provided by Governor Lachlan Macquarie. It has since become known as Westpac.

In the USA a significant centralization of international money power through the trading banks came with the creation of the privately owned Federal Reserve Bank in the United States of America in 1913.

The international Brenton Woods Agreement made in 1944 required all countries to peg their currencies to a certain amount of gold. Although in practice, most currencies were pegged to the U.S. Dollar, which was itself pegged to gold. The Agreement worked relatively well until the United States unilaterally depegged from gold in 1971. (*Source: Farlex Financial Dictionary. © 2009 Farlex, Inc.*)

Now virtually all economies use privately issued bank credit as their main money supply. This is supplemented by fiat currency; notes and coins that are made legal tender by government decree.

For the common good to be served the need is for an alternative to the private issue of bank credit because the issue of private bank credit simultaneously creates social debt, owed back to the banks.

Repayment of debts using the existing money supply will cause the money supply to contract, as deposits must be withdrawn or cash returned to the bank, which removes the cash from circulation. To top up the money supply (money stock) new money needs to be issued but using bank credit, issued as interest bearing debt, is inflationary.

Also an expansion of the money supply using new credit issued as interest bearing debt contributes to inflation.

The reverse is also true. A decrease in the money supply will be deflationary. If loans are paid back faster than new loans are issued then the money supply must contract. A reduction in the money supply is deflationary and the known consequences of such periods are recession, depression, misery, bankruptcy and suicides.

No one, allegedly living by "The Golden Rule" of doing unto others as they would have others do unto them, could seriously advocate deflationary finance policies to solve the debt problem. Certainly the community neither wants nor will benefit from further recessions or depressions.

The world as a whole can never borrow itself out of debt. Borrowed money can never cancel total debts so there is no redemption from debt, not when the only way to obtain the credit needed to pay the debts is to borrow it and so create more debt. This is the ultimate Catch 22 and at present we are in it.

5. How can we all get out of debt?

Strange as it may seem, the only way to solve the debt problem is to issue more money, but not as loans and definitely not as interest bearing loans.

The additional money needed to reduce total debt must be issued, not as a loan but as a gift, which by definition is free of debt and interest.

Acts 20:35 "... remember the words of Yeshua the Messiah (Jesus Christ), that He Himself said, 'It is more blessed to give than to receive.'"

This brings us to a consideration of two fundamental questions.

Who should own the community's money supply as it is created? We should already know that it must be created both debt and interest free otherwise it will cause inflation and an expansion of total debt.

Contenders for the Ownership of All New Money.

This is a very important matter.

The money supply is usually taken to mean the existing store of money, as measured by bank deposits and currency in the hands of the public.

But there is another aspect to the *money supply* which needs to be addressed and that is; from whom does the community, obtain its money supply?

Reserve Bank figures show that our supply of physical currency, notes and coins in circulation, has not increased significantly, over the past few years. It is steady at about forty-five billion dollars ($45,000,000,000).

However new financial credit is being issued as loans by the trading banks continuously and this rate considerably exceeds the rate of loan repayments so the money supply is steadily rising. The amounts are astonishing but the average yearly increase over the last 10 years in Australia is over $3,500 per person.

So the crucial question is. Who is the rightful owner of money that is yet to be created? There are three obvious contenders for the ownership of new financial credit; the private banks, the government or the citizens.

The Private Banks.

No change to the present system.

Ownership of all new financial credit stays with those who keep the books and issue the credit, i.e. the trading banks. Proof of their claim of ownership is evidenced by the fact that the main way this money is issued is by way of interest bearing loans. Be it to individual Australian citizens, companies or governments, it is nearly always a loan and usually at the highest possible interest rate.

By claiming all new financial credit as their own the banks have usurped each citizen's legitimate share of the nation's money supply as it is created.

The Government.

The government is another contender for the ownership of all new money. The Federal or State Governments are obvious contenders. Obviously they see to it that they could use this new money any way they see fit.

Do you trust the government to act in your best interest or its own? Wouldn't the government be more likely to grow and become less and less responsive to the will of the people?

The Citizens.

New money would no longer belong to the banks, it would belong to the citizens.

In this case the distribution of new money, created in Australia, would be distributed free of tax, debt and interest charges to the Australian citizens.

The main exception to this would be that portion of new money issued as a consumer subsidy to reduce the price of local production. The subsidy would primarily function to reduce the cost to the consumer at a rate that will accurately reflect the physical cost of production. The subsidy would also prevent inflation and counter unfair competition from various countries that exploit their populations with inhuman working conditions to export cheap products.

6. Money in Australia.

In Australia and throughout the world, the creation of financial credit using the debt based system is expanding the money supply but at the same time expanding world debt.

This phenomenon is occurring at an increasing rate. For example the annual rate of the expansion of the money supply in Australia during the five years from 1987 to 1992 averaged about $1,125 per head of population. This amount was equivalent to about 3 week's wages for an adult shop assistant. This credit was issued as an asset of the banks and a debt to the community. Being issued as a debt, the debt obligation must flow into the national price structure at varying rates and so cause price rises, which will be needed to fund the repayment of the debts plus interest.

The present operation of the financial system makes inflation a mathematic certainty because it issues money into circulation in such a way as to cause a corresponding or greater increase in prices, which is inflation. Inflation is a deliberate design feature of the current system.

The following graph shows the growth in the money supply over the 10 years up to 2012. The graph is created from published Reserve Bank of Australia figures and shows the monthly growth of Australia's money supply in billions of dollars.

10 years of M3 and Currency growth in Australia

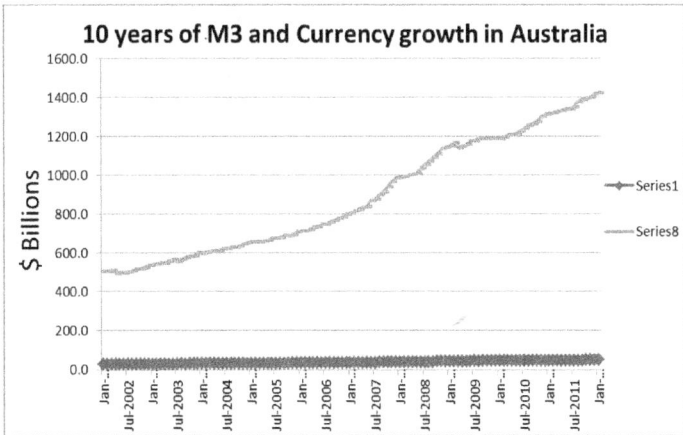

Series 8 is M3 and Series 1 is Currency.

(*Source:* www.rba.gov.au/statistics/tables/ Then find: MONETARY AGGREGATES)

The graph shows that over the 10 year period 2002 through 2012 the M3 monetary aggregate of money in Australia increased by $918.2 billion Australian dollars; from $505.4 billion to $1,422.6 billion. Only two percent of the $908.2 billion increase consisted of an increase in currency, which grew by $22.7 billion. This is an amount that would be hardly significant except that it factually shows that the government wasn't actually "running the printing presses" as is commonly portrayed by finance commentators in the media. It is a moot point who claimed ownership of the face value of the $22.7 billion in extra currency.

The average growth of the money supply over the ten years was therefore $91.82 billion per year, which could have alternatively financed a payment to every citizen of just over $4,000 every year. Put another way the payment to the average family of dad, mum and a couple of children could have been about $1,333 per month. Now that would sure reduce mortgage stress!

One can arrived at these amounts by doing some simple yet revealing mathematics. Divide the average annual increase in the money supply by the number of citizens, which in March 2012 in Australia was 22,858,609 people.

(Source:
www.abs.gov.au/ausstats/abs@.nsf/0/1647509ef7e25 faaca2568a900154b63?OpenDocument*)*

$91,820,000,000 divided by 22,858,609 people.

The result is $4,016.90 each.

Given that the average population during the last 10 years is smaller than it is now, the annual four thousand dollars per person amount is actually an under estimate.

The per capita on expansion in M3 over the twelve months prior to March 2012 was $4,396.56 which is over $366 per month to each person.

The increase in the money supply consisted entirely of "new deposits", almost all created and issued as loans by the banking system.

I use the term "**new deposits**" as distinct from **transferred deposits**. Transferred deposits don't increase the total money supply. Every transferred deposit is matched by a corresponding withdrawal of some other deposit; such as when using a debit card or electronic funds transfer between deposit accounts. These are virtually the same as paying for something with cash. The transactions have no effect on the volume of money.

New deposits come from all transactions that use newly issued bank credit. These new deposits are not counter balanced by any withdrawal and are usually created in exchange for debts owed to the deposit authorising bank.

Imagine if you can what this country would be like now if the expansion in the Australian money supply over the past 10 years had been distributed evenly to all the citizens as dividends and subsidies rather than created and issued as interest bearing debt.

It is important to realise that Commonwealth or State Dividend payments to all citizens would be in addition to all other sources of income.

A Commonwealth Dividend would have relieved, if not eliminated, "mortgage stress" and unnecessary poverty in Australia.

The dividend payments to citizens must not be borrowed into existence. The money should be paid into existence as interest and debt free deposits to all citizens.

The reserve bank figures quoted above, only record the net effect on deposits.

In actual fact, the amount of new deposits created by the commercial banks must have been far greater than that which caused the growth in the money supply by nearly $800 billion over the past ten years.

Over the same 10 year period regular commercial bank loan repayments occurred as people paid down their mortgages and reduced their personal indebtedness. Such repayments would have had the effect of reducing total deposits had not additional trading bank loans created replacement deposits during the same period. Debt repayments when funded by new loans do not affect the volume of money just as, in the same way; borrowing more to pay debt doesn't reduce total debt.

The loans by trading banks that created deposits to balance loan repayments during the ten year period were additional to the loan created deposits that caused the rise in the M3 figures.

So for example, if a million families and businesses paid down their indebtedness to the trading banks by $1,000 per month for a year then $12 billion would need to be issued as new loans just to keep the volume of money from shrinking during that year.

The figures I've seen don't disclose the amount representing debts repaid and new loans issued. However, for there to have been a net average yearly increase of $91.82 billion on top of all repayments, then the actual bank issued credit money would have been far greater than the net figure discussed thus far.

If one accepts that the expansion of the money supply should be issued as dividends and distributed to the citizens, rather than issued as debt and loaned to them; the same principle would logically apply to all other credit issued by the private commercial trading bank system.

From what we have seen so far it may be apparent that a significant part of the heavy financial yoke imposed by financial orthodoxy can be lifted from the Australian community by distributing to each citizen their fair share of all newly issued money.

As citizens, we need to instruct our political representatives, especially those in the Commonwealth Parliament, to once again regulate the banking system and instruct the Reserve Bank to progressively raise the fractional reserve ratio for all banks to unity, i.e. 100%. The Reserve Bank should then be instructed to supply to all citizens of Australia their fair and equal share of all new money needed to maintain or expand the money supply for the commonweal (benefit of all).

At present the commercial trading banks create and control the distribution of the Australian money supply. Money is only made available to the community in exchange for interest bearing debt, unless it is used to pay interest on deposits or finance bank acquisitions of goods and services.

The crucial question is who should be the rightful owners of all newly created Australian money?

At present, ownership of all new money is granted to the trading banks.

The answer as to how much money should be issued will be for some State or National Credit Issuing Authority to get right. It may be the Reserve Bank unless it is already privatised.

The writer believes that the ownership of all new money issued in Australia, must be resolved in favour of every individual Australian citizen. A share of all new money would be regularly issued to each citizen. This would take the form of a national dividend, a credit with no interest bearing debt attached.

By way of explanation, it is the social and physical economy that enables the present work force to produce real credit, in the form of capital equipment, inventions, goods and services. This social infrastructure is the product of the efforts of generations of citizens in the past and is our cultural heritage, a group inheritance. The national dividend is the financial counterpart of our physical inheritance.

One of the functions of money is that it is supposed to act as a measure of value. Bank credit has corrupted this function. To re-establish this basic function of money there must be a dynamic balance between the total goods and services available in the community, and the total money supply. As is with the case with theatre tickets, there must be sufficient tickets to utilise with the number of seats. So a reasonable conclusion is that there needs to be issued, sufficient money to enable the community as a whole to purchase the total available goods and services within the nation without incurring debt. This is a dynamic relationship and relates directly to total production and consumption within the community.

The purpose of the production system is, as the writer and many others see it, to produce, on demand the goods and service wanted by individuals expressing their free will in the community. Production should be in the most efficient possible way and with the least amount of waste, both of human time and natural resources.

Consumer goods would once again be designed to last years, and when people are not artificially short of money, they can afford to buy quality. Low quality producers would not be supported by consumers and would go out of production, but not into poverty or destitution.

The greatest, in the sense of most skilled, most inventive, most efficient would serve the community and be well rewarded. There would be sufficient purchasing power (money) distributed to enable even displaced workers in the community to consume the production of the machines that displaced them from their labour. The production system will continue to become more automated but in an accelerating rate because there will be no disincentive motivated by fear of unemployment and possible poverty. The policy of full employment can be declared redundant. There will be more time for working out ways to do what we already do, even more efficiently. Those not needed in the production system would be secure to pursue other personal and cultural goals, in an environment of expanding freedom and liberty.

The most capable producers will emerge as the greatest. Their greatness will be because they are best at serving the community of consumers.

In the Bible the book of *Mark 10:42-45 Yeshua (Jesus) called them together and said, "You know that those who are regarded as rulers of the Gentiles lord it over them, and their high officials exercise authority over them. Not so with you. Instead, whoever wants to become great among you must be your servant, and whoever wants to be first must be slave of all. For even the Son of Man did not come to be served, but to serve, and to give his life as a ransom for many." (NIV)*

The economy must adhere to this same principal of the greatest serving, if it is to be successful. This would in practice be Biblical Economic Democracy. If we achieve this the citizens as a whole and not the bankers, will control the policy and direction of the production system. The share market will have plenty of investors.

At present any society or individual who wishes to be out of debt will also be out of credit and if not out of credit, will have shifted the burden of debt to others.

7. The Douglas Discoveries.

The financial proposals of the Late C. H. Douglas, who coined the term Social Credit, will probably prove to be the only financial policy that is close enough to the truth to work. The truth will set us all free. Douglas had sufficient insight to penetrate the deceptive mystery of the debt based finance system and proposed an astonishing solution to the debt problem.

The Social Credit School of Studies has a wealth of information on the subject. www.ecn.net.au/~socred/

C. H. Douglas realised that no business could pay its workers and shareholders enough money to enable these people (workers and bosses) to purchase all the products and services that their business produced over any period of time, unless the business was trading at a loss.

For example, the weekly gross takings of a small restaurant could be distributed as follows: 30% wages, 30% product purchases, 30% business overheads and 10% profit for the owner. So the purchasing power distributed to individuals is 40% of the total cost of the finished products.

The economy of an entire nation is just a large scale version of the same scenario. The production system can't distribute sufficient purchasing power to enable the actual producers to consume their own production on an ongoing basis.

Taxing workers to provide additional purchasing power to the unemployed is totally futile. It doesn't address the basic problem, which is that there is insufficient disposable income (i.e. purchasing power), in the hands of the community to purchase all the goods and services they are capable of producing, that is unless they go into debt.

Douglas predicted that the consequences of issuing money as interest bearing debt will be escalating debt and social disintegration.

He developed precise proposals to solve the problem of insufficient purchasing power in the hands of the individual citizens.

Eliminating Debt with Dividend Payments.

He proposed the issue, to all citizens, of a national dividend and the use of consumer subsidies to reduce the price of goods and services by a rate that accurately reflected the physical efficiency of the production system. The subsidy would reduce the price to the consumer to what Douglas called, "The Just Price".

The Douglas proposals were intended to bring about a just financial system that served every individual and thus benefit the whole community.

The currency issuing system would be democratised to serve and benefit all citizens.

Douglas presented these proposals to the bankers of his time. The mathematical accuracy of his assessment could not be faulted but they opposed any reduction of power they derived from their monopoly over the nation's money supply.

Leading bankers knew they had the monopoly over the issue of financial credit and with this monopoly they effectively controlled all that could be done with the power of money. Their reaction was understandable.

No money was spared in ongoing attempts to prevent the proposals ever seeing the light of day. Those associated with the idea were smeared and ridiculed. The proposals were mockingly called "funny money". How hypocritical; as if the existing system doesn't issue funny money!

Social Credit has even been mistakenly described as some type of socialism. The policy of Socialism is monopoly and centralisation of power. The goal: total centralised power over the society. The whole left-wing, right-wing political paradigm is Socialist. Extreme left is Communism (International Socialism); the extreme right is Nazism (National Socialism) in the centre are the so-called moderates, the Fabian Socialists that are misguidedly attempting to achieve the same centralisation of power by stealth. This whole winged political creature is heading to a centralised hell with policy making in the hands of some elite group. In Australia it seems that whenever socialist political parties gain power they deliberately attempt to sink the society in debt and destroy any State bank if one happens to exist. They consistently behave like agents for the private commercial bankers.

The fundamental error of socialism is that both policy and administration are centralised. Big Brother determines the policy and does it. The centralising of policy and its administration must yield bad fruit and eventually fail because the concentration of power breeds corruption. Social credit by advocating decentralised policy is the exact opposite of Socialism yet it is not Capitalism.

Policy and Administration.

The man who realised the potential of the Social Credit, C.H. Douglas, also had revealing insights into the correct relationship between policy and administration.

Policy describes what is wanted, whereas administration is the organisational structure necessary to achieve the fulfilment of policy.

Yeshua the Messiah (Jesus Christ) taught His disciples that he who desires to be greatest must be a servant (slave) to all, see...

Mat 20:27 "And whoever desires to be first among you, let him be your slave-- (NKJ)

Mark 10:44 "And whoever of you desires to be first shall be slave of all."

Individuals who serve the community earn the highest awards. For one who seeks to serve, it is vitally important to learn the wants and needs of those whom you are seeking to serve.

One obvious way that people show what they want is how they spend their money. Every purchase is a prioritised policy decision. The purchase is also indicative of the need for a replacement product.

Policy is the desired outcome; it is what is wanted. Policy must be determined individually and thus is automatically decentralised. Those who start a business often perceive a need in the community.

Profitably serving the consumers' need is the purpose of the business. The most successful businesses satisfy the wants of the most people.

Administration however must be hierarchical. Administration is the organisational structure that is required in a business or any other organisation to achieve the policy goals of the organisation. The leader, so long as he is endeavouring to achieve the agreed policy, must command a structure that follows orders. Clearly the organisation of the administrative structure must be hierarchical if the policy is to be achieved. The leader is responsible both for the methods used to achieve the policy and the results. They must have sufficient authority and resources to function. However those involved in the hierarchy must have the option of freely contracting out.

Constitutional Democracy is an attempt to ensure that the administration (government) serves the policy of the electorate. The constitution is the only constraint upon the power of the administration. Governments typically try to work around constitutional limitations.

Democracy would be enhanced by providing for a Voter's Veto, which is a mechanism to address the age old problem that the instruments of government may implement policies that are not the policy of the community. Politicians are supposed to be representative of their electorate who's moral duty is to re-present their electors' policy. All too often elected representatives are just party delegates and as such they serve the policy of the party, not the policy of their electors.

In summary: policy must be decentralised, administration must be centralised.

Producers and Consumers.

Generally people are both producers and consumers. Whether one is a producer or a consumer depends on the time of life, of year, of season, of day. Sometimes we produce, sometimes we consume and often we do both.

Producers and consumers need each other. They interact in the market. Consumers give orders (policy) and producers carry them out (administration).

Some sort of inducement is normally needed; it can be anything in a range from love through to fear. Money functions as an emotionally neutral intermediary that is so successful that it is money that is usually the inducement offered. Money establishes the credibility of an order for goods and services with the producer. In the world of business and economics, an order becomes effective demand if it can be backed up with sufficient money to complete the transaction. Often a deposit or down payment is required.

The greatest producers will be those who best produce the goods and services which the members of the community order, both individually and collectively.

Producers and consumers are the market.

Potential consumers usually have a fair idea of what they want but money is usually the limitation. Without sufficient money potential consumers are only window shopping because being unfunded, they can't purchase. However when consumers are not short of money, what consumers then need are producers who can provide them with the goods and services they want; when and where, they want them.

What about the producers? Producers mainly want customers (consumers) who want their product and who have the money to back up their desires. The capacity of a person to consume what is offered in the market is essentially limited by two factors: (1) desire for what is offered and; (2) the money to pay for it.

So producers want consumers with money and would be consumers want money so they can make purchases.

The only mechanism that is hindering everyone's satisfaction is the commercial trading banking that issue and control the money supply for its own undeniably devilish ends.

John 10:10 NKJ " "The thief comes only to steal, and kill, and destroy; I (Yeshua) came that they might have life, and might have it abundantly. "

Consumption – Production's Cost and Purpose.

Consumption is the real purpose of production.

There is no other legitimate reason to produce anything other than so that it may be of service to consumers.

Consumption is also the real cost of production.

The physical cost of production is consumption, which is the value of whatever was consumed during production. Consumption is the actual physical cost of anything. A simple example may help. Supposing one grain of wheat grows to become a plant producing one head of wheat at harvest. Question: What was the physical cost of the head of wheat at harvest? Answer: The one grain of wheat, which ceased to exist and minuscule quantities of recycled minerals, air and water. All of which came free with the planet.

The increase during production is a gift.

Increase is difference between the value of the product and the value of what was consumed whilst producing it. Increase is the physical profit from production.

1Corinthians 3:7 (NKJ) So then neither he who plants is anything, nor he who waters, but God who gives the increase.

Note: God gives the increase, He doesn't lend it.

1Corinthians 3:8 Now he who plants and he who waters are one, and each one will receive his own reward according to his own labour.

Note: Those who work in the production system are paid and worthy of their wages. Both Luke 10:7 and 1Tim 6:1 also confirm this teaching.

Work may be done voluntarily. Obviously one doesn't need to be in paid employment to be a willing worker and productively engaged. When someone is physically secure, say because of a large inheritance or a lottery win that person has no need to seek employment to obtain money. Such a one may nevertheless do considerable amounts of work. Such voluntary work is simply unpaid employment activity. Depending on the individual this unpaid employment may be selfish or philanthropic. So anyone may choose to enhancing the community as a volunteer so long as their money supply lasts.

What of the increase? The increase is the physical profit of the production system. The production system as a whole was given to us by and through our forefathers. It is our cultural inheritance.

Cultural Inheritance.

The ability of our culture to arrange our production system to yield an increase is largely an inherited capacity. We inherited the essentials; the language, communication, know how, transportation systems; water, food and electricity supplies. Without our cultural inheritance we could not be as productive and may not even survive.

The idea of providing something for nothing irks some people who don't trust others with un-earned income. They express concern about what other people will do with their dividend. Such people should consider well what the apostle Paul said, *Romans 14:10 (NKJ) But why do you judge your brother? Or why do you show contempt for your brother? For we shall all stand before the judgment seat of Messiah.*

What is the promise given to those who overcome? The promise is that they shall **inherit** all things. It is interesting to note that one of the ten points in the Communist Manifesto is the elimination of all right of inheritance. The exact opposite of God's will.

As we are all members of the community then we are all inheritors of the progress and abundance produced by our predecessors.

It must also be kept in mind that without the efforts of generations of citizens producing the real credit, in the form of goods and services, financial credit would have no value. Money has no value in an empty market.

National Dividends to All Citizens.

The national dividend is not to be financed out of taxation nor Government borrowing. It is to be a new issue of money, which is what all bank credit is anyway. However this time no interest bearing debt is to be created.

The consumers need to receive enough debt free purchasing power to prevent the production system from running out of effective demand. Effective demand is a purchase order backed up by sufficient financial credit to complete the transaction.

An example of insufficient debt free purchasing power in the hands of the public is the unpaid credit card debt carried over at the end of each monthly cycle. The goods and services were available but not the money. Credit card debt is but the tip of the proverbial iceberg of debt.

What Is Your Share Worth?

How much money would need to be issued and equitably distributed to the citizens?

The amount each citizen should receive is not a fixed amount and its monthly calculation a technical point, but the amount is surely not beyond the wit of our society to determine. It would need to be publically and transparently calculated and distributed equitably.

For a start, the volume of new credit would need to be sufficient to balance out the total internal debt of the community.

So we could reasonably total up the national debt and start to issue it as a credit, preferably equally, to all citizens. This proposal is a much fairer way to get rid of the community's debt than the often mooted alternative of writing off the debts of a few selected bank customers. Selectively writing of debts is the most unfair way to address the problem, as it leaves enormous and corrupting power in the hands of those deciding whose debts will be forgiven and this would allow the present immorality to continue.

How much is your share worth? In Australia it is over sixty thousand dollars.

How do we determine this figure? Given that, as was quoted earlier; "all money is a debt of the banking system", we can use the RBA's M3 aggregate and the present population.

The M3 monetary aggregate figure from the RBA in Australia as at February 29th, 2012 was $1,422.6 billion and the population mid-March is 22,858,609. Dividing the M3 figure by the population results in an amount of $62,236.70 each, this amount is up from around $54,000 in mid-2010. So in the previous 20 month the banking system has increased the Australian money supply on average by over $410 per person each month and claimed the lot as its own. The money was then lent to whomever it liked.

To rectify this situation money (debt cancelling credit) should be released steadily freely to the citizens at the rate of bank debt redemption. The new money will maintain the money supply at its current level whilst progressively eliminating both bank debt and the interest cost burden that the borrowed money supply generated.

Many citizens could use all their share of the credit in debt clearing and still have debt left over; so for these people who have already borrowed more than their share of the nation's credit; they would need to continue to serve the general community, supplying goods and services to earn enough to repay their debts. The good thing is that they would be offering their services to consumers who would be well cashed up. As for those prudent folk who don't have more than their share of the national debt, they could perhaps consider taking a well-earned holiday break.

So far we have only considered issuing sufficient new credit to balance out the existing debt.

More will need to be distributed.

Again, let me explain. Money is supposed to act as a stable measure of value. For this to be true there must be a dynamic balance between the total goods and services available in the community, and the total money supply. Just as in the case of boarding passes issued for a flight, there is an exact number required at any particular time.

This brings us to the reasonable conclusion that there needs to be issued, sufficient money to enable the community to purchase the total available goods and services within the economy without incurring debt.

This is a dynamic relationship and relates directly to total production and consumption within the community. More goods and services require more issued credit to maintain the balance. If total production falls below total consumption then the money supply logically needs to be restricted. A simple way to do this would be to reduce the consumer subsidy discount rate.

Understanding Inflation.

There is a common but erroneous belief that the creation and issue of money contributes to inflation. This belief is based on a simple "dilution theory". It falsely assumes there is already the correct amount of money in circulation to purchase all the goods and services available but this is obviously not the case. It also ignores the money cancelling effect of debt repayments. Inflation is not necessarily caused by an increase in the volume of money unless the terms of issue of the money causes an increase in the cost of production. Then prices must eventually rise.

The primary cause of inflation is new financial credit (money) entering circulation in such a way that it must be accounted for as a cost to both producers and consumers. For example, inflation is initiated when additional bank credit is loaned to producers. The producers must include the debt and interest charges as part of their cost of production. The resulting products must be priced high enough to enable principle repayments and interest charges. The same applies to bank credit loaned to workers who will need to use more of their income to repay the loan plus interest.

The terms and conditions of loan repayment will determine the effect on prices. Long term low interest loans cause less inflationary pressure than short term high interest loans.

One of the most illogical standard policies routinely implemented by central banks is to raise interest rates in response to rising inflation. Higher interest rates must increase the cost of production and thus cause inflation.

Economists blindly trapped in the dilution theory think that higher interest rates reduce borrowing and therefore reduce the volume of money. When money is scarcer, they reason it will buy more. But what is actually happening is that consumers have less disposable income so sales slow. Desperate producers lower prices in an attempt to secure sales, even at a loss, just to pay their debts and hopefully avoid bankruptcy. Sure prices may fall but at horrendous social costs with layoffs and bankruptcies.

The practice of raising interest rates to control inflation is a totally inappropriate way to control inflation and apparently senseless. However central bank policies make much more sense when one looks at them from the point of view of bankers, who get others to build bank approved assets during booms, after which the banks confiscate the assets during the bust part of the boom and bust cycles that bank practices cause.

It is worth noting that the policies imposed by international banks on nations in financial difficulties will invariably require; reduced government spending and balancing the budget, which usually means, reducing services, raising taxes and eliminating of all consumer subsidies, in short; austerity measures.

Stopping Inflation with New Money.

Consumer subsidies lower prices.

During the Second World War in Australia enormous amounts of new money was spent into circulation in the form of government contracts and wages. The extra purchasing power could have "bid up prices" but prices to consumers were prevented from rising by the use of consumer subsidies. Consumer subsidies are like sales taxes in reverse. As a direct result of the use of consumer subsidies, inflation ceased for the period that subsidies were issued. So the practice of using consumer subsidies as an effective means of controlling inflation has already been proven to work in this country.

The Commonwealth Year Book of 1946-47, page 461, in the chapter "Control of Prices" explains under heading 9, Treatment of Costs and Subsidies, how this was done:

"When increased costs could not be absorbed within the process by production or distribution they were met generally at the source by payment of subsidies and thus prevented from disturbing the whole price structure."

http://www.alor.org/Political%20Democracy/They%20
Want%20Your%20Land.htm

The consumer subsidies were financed with the same new financial credit source that financed government contracts for armaments; namely long term, low interest war bonds financed by the commercial trading banks.

I recall my late father telling me that his bank manager asked him to buy war bonds. When my father questioned the cost, the manager told him that the bank would lend him the money to buy the war bonds. So the commercial banks created the money as new credit, loaned it to their customers who purchased the government bonds. The appearance was that the citizens were financing the war effort, although in reality the banks were creating all the money that the government needed. I believe people sold their jewellery to supposedly finance the war effort. – What a swindle that was.

The ratio of consumer subsidies.

Ultimately the rate of subsidy should match the efficiency of the total production system. This is technically a simple matter, and its use will eliminate inflation for ever. As efficiency increases so will the subsidy. The subsidy should not be financed from taxation but from new issues of money for the purpose. New money but definitely not borrowed at interest from the private banks.

For any technical minds the actual ratio of the subsidy is exactly the same as the ratio of national production to national consumption.

Achieving Stable Just Prices.

When we as a community produce what we want more efficiently, prices should logically fall but current banking practices reverse the logical.

When new money is issued, without interest bearing debt and at the correct rate, there will be no financial imperative for prices to rise. Prices will also fall as a result of the application of consumer price subsidies.

Prices can be expected to fall gradually as a result of increasing efficiency and technology, rather than progressively rise through artificially created and deliberately manipulated monetary inflation.

Wages, Salaries & Dividends.

The production system obviously needs decreasing input of human energy to function efficiently. So wages will represent a decreasing proportion of the cost of production.

One of the fundamental problems is that in any given period of time the combined wages, salaries and dividends distributed by any business cannot purchase any more than a shrinking proportion of the goods and services produced by the business during that period of time.

Wages, salaries and dividends are practically the total purchasing power of the consumers, unless consumers go into debt. The Bible in Romans 13:8 councils against owing anyone anything except love. It seems reasonable to interpret this as advice teaching us to stay out of debt.

Now, in any given period of time, the combined wages, salaries and dividends paid to individuals in the community is insufficient to purchase ALL the goods and services they have produced during that same period. This situation, is simply explained because the wages, salaries and dividends will be included as part of the minimum market price because they are part of the cost of production for that period. All profitable businesses must market their product at or above the cost of production. The only exception is if the price is subsidised.

In the nation as a whole, only that shrinking proportion of production that is equivalent to wages, salaries and dividends can be purchased without drawing on some other source of money. This extra money will and must be issued. Who owns it as and to whom it is issued is the heart of the matter.

Currently, because all money is a debt to the banking system, any debt free money you have will either be the result of payments received for your products or services; redistributed taxation, interest earnings or share dividends. In all cases someone else will be carrying the debt and interest charges.

Who wouldn't prefer to freely receive their fair share of all new releases of Australian money? This would be your own share of the Social Credit dividend and consumer subsidy benefit. The choice is yours. Your personal freedom and liberty will depend on your choice and your preparedness to act on your choice.

Asset Depreciation & Credit Cancellation.

For the rate of issue and cancellation of financial credit to reflect reality the depreciation of assets must be taken into account. The concept of writing down and eventually writing off assets is not unusual. The depreciation of national assets must be accounted for in such a way that will reduce, by a corresponding amount, the new money to be issued.

Determining the rate to write off assets must be true. Depreciation must be factored into the cost of production for determination of the just price to charge for the consumptive use of the asset. Depreciation rates should match the actual rate of depreciation of assets. Artificially accelerated depreciation is a falsehood used to reduce income tax. From a national accounting perspective the result of accelerated depreciation is real national assets with no book value.

8. Leisure, Work, Liberty and Progress.

Leisure.

Leisure is not necessarily rest, and leisure is not necessarily laziness.

It is an unfortunate error to assume that there is something inherently evil in leisure. A person with little faith, will fear what other people will do if they have more leisure.

Perhaps we need to define leisure.

Leisure is the economic condition of **voluntary activity**.

Strenuous activity may be done voluntarily, plenty of people do "workouts" in a gym. Obviously one doesn't need to be in paid employment to be a willing worker and productively engaged. When someone is physically secure, say because of a large inheritance or a lottery win that person has no need to seek employment to obtain money. Such a one may nevertheless do considerable amounts of work. Such voluntary work is simply unpaid employment activity. Depending on the individual this unpaid employment may be selfish or philanthropic. So anyone may choose to enhancing the community as a volunteer so long as their money supply lasts.

Work.

Work (labour) not being voluntary is **forced activity**, requiring "inducement".

There are broadly two types of work.

NATURAL WORK.

Natural Work is necessary and of some dignity. It is work imposed by the natural environment. The native bushman who must daily hunt for survival is not undignified.

ARTIFICIAL WORK.

Artificial Work is forced upon us by other men. Artificial work is unnecessary, undignified, and servile. This may also be considered as un-Godly work.

When a society is serving Mammon the likely result is a high proportion of un-Godly work.

Liberty.

Liberty amounts to freedom from servile labour.

Individually Man has always striven for Liberty, being freedom from servile labour.

Progress.

Progress is simply freedom from Nature forced work. Progress is collective in its distinctiveness.

Collectively mankind has always striven for progress, freedom from Nature forced activity.

All collective progress has been accomplished by relatively free individuals and teams. Most progress comes from investing time and resources into research and development (R&D). This needs uncommitted resources and individual liberty.

We owe our Collective Progress to Individual Liberty.

The Fruit of Progress

Progress offers the following options:

Unemployment - a leisure lifestyle without financial security or servility waiting for a servile job.

War - Full employment making products to supply, free of charge, to people who do not want them. War is a form of "forced consumption".

or

Leisure - economically guaranteed voluntary activity for all.

Leisure is With a Social Credit National or State Dividend there will be no need to export war and our swords can be hammered into plow shears in fulfilment of two famous Messianic Biblical prophecies.

Isaiah 2:4 He shall judge between the nations, And rebuke many people; They shall beat their swords into ploughshares, And their spears into pruning hooks; Nation shall not lift up sword against nation, Neither shall they learn war anymore.

Micah 4:3 He shall judge between many peoples, And rebuke strong nations afar off; They shall beat their swords into ploughshares, And their spears into pruning hooks; Nation shall not lift up sword against nation, Neither shall they learn war any more.

9. Fallacious Economic Policies.

The financial problem we have is that we can't purchase all the goods we, as a community, made ourselves without going into debt.

The equitable distribution of production is not a physical problem, it is an administrative one. The problem is really how to distribute God's abundance. The community needs an additional supply of money for all the goods and services to be profitably and equitably distributed for consumption.

Several plausible pseudo solutions are in vogue to solve the problem of insufficient debt free purchasing power. None of the following solves the problem; they are all fallacious policies because none challenge the claim by the commercial trading banks to the ownership of all new money, so these policies were accepted in ignorance.

- Full Employment.
- Increase wages.
- Export more and import less.
- More foreign investment
- More tourists
- More consumer loans.
- Work harder.
- Produce more.
- Save more.
- Consume less.
- Austerity.

The Full Employment Fallacy.

The call for full employment is more to do with the need for people to have a secure income than a genuine desire to be working for someone else. If the entire workforce was fully employed in genuine production the problem would quickly become a problem of glut.

The fallacy of the full employment policy should by now be obvious. As stated earlier, it is impossible for the combined salaries, wages and dividends distributed to all producers during any given period of time to purchase what they have produced during that same period of time. This is because what they receive is only a part of the cost of production and hence part of the selling price.

Technological advances are reducing the need for human labour in the production process. This is progress. However the policy of those with a monopoly over money creation denies community access to the output of the technological machine age except in return for unredeemable social debt and wage slavery.

In the Biblical account of creation the first man Adam was put in the Garden of Eden to *freely* eat and tend the garden. The use of the word tend may be considered in a similar way to how one tends a piece of production machinery, it does all the heavy work and we take care of it.

Genesis 2:15 NKJ Then the Lord God took the man and put him in the Garden of Eden to tend and keep it. 16 And the Lord God commanded the man, saying, "Of every tree of the garden you may freely eat; ...

After "the fall" the ground was cursed and man was compelled to toil all the days of his life. Note: ALL the days; no mention of rest here.

Gen 3:17 "Cursed is the ground because of you; through painful toil you will eat of it all the days of your life. 18 It will produce thorns and thistles for you, and you will eat the plants of the field. 19 By the sweat of your brow you will eat your food until you return to the ground."

Adam was to be fully employed because he was under a curse. Full employment as a policy, is derived from this curse.

The curse started to be lifted with the reestablishment of the weekly day of rest, the Shabbat (Sabbath). The Shabbat was instigated through Moshe (Moses) after he was obedient and led the Children of Israel out of Egypt. In Egypt they were slaves 24/7. A day off once a week was presumably a big improvement and a foretaste of things to come eventually.

Full employment seems to assume people must be employed by other people in exchange for money to be worthy to receive access to the output of the production system.

The most common periods of full employment is during war and during reconstruction immediately after war. At these times the producers are not expected to purchase the total production with their wages because the government borrows the money to finance the orders.

The only Biblical reference to full or continual employment is when men were required to bury all the slain after a war that is probably yet to be fought in the Middle East. The reference is in Ezekiel 39:14.

The Increase Wages Fallacy.

Increasing wages can't solve the problem as the increased wages cause an even greater rise in prices.

Supposing total wages are increased by one billion dollars. To pay the higher wages industry must borrow an additional one billion dollars to pay this new cost. Interest charges on the borrowed money will force a total price rise of one billion plus interest charges. However the wage earners get the billion LESS tax.

The net result in this example is that prices rise by one billion plus interest, and the purchasing power of the workers increases by one billion less tax. The problem is not solved, but made worse.

The Export More and Import Less Fallacy.

Exporting more goods than we import is called achieving "A FAVOURABLE BALANCE OF TRADE". Favourable to whom? Not us! If we export more value than we import then we are physically impoverished. Who are we supposed to export to? Our cultural allies generally aren't short of produce, because they have the same problem that we have, namely a shortage of cashed up customers. The most likely result is that we end up exporting to our cultural enemies.

Why do it? The basic idea is that we use the surplus financial credit left after paying for imports to enable us to consume our un-exported surplus production. The resulting trade surplus is also intended to help get us out of foreign debt.

Imports are seen as somewhat financially undesirable because imports flood a market already short of purchasing power. There is also the problem that imports contribute to unemployment which undermines the full employment policy.

Nearly all countries are undertaking massive export programs in a futile, though sincere attempt to export their economy out of debt or maybe to pay interest on their existing debt. Excessive export of manufactured goods and primary production like timber, minerals and agricultural products, are the cause of much of the exploitation and pollution of the environment.

Unfortunately this is current doctrine in orthodox economics but the "Favourable Balance of Trade" policy is simply a very plausible illusion.

Note: Financing the excess of exports over imports is done by a slight of hand procedure within international finance. The money the exporter receives payment in is locally created Australian dollars. However from the point of view of the exporter, a deposit ends up in his account, so he is satisfied. When we look at the economy as a whole, local credit is issued because goods were removed (by export) from the market. Orthodox economics maintains that "more money chasing less goods" contributes to inflation.

The More Foreign Investment Fallacy.

So-called foreign investment results in the creation of new deposits (new money) within the local banking system without the creation of any more local debt. Foreign investments are also encouraged because they also create more employment. However we could just as easily create the same money and also not "sell the farm".

The More Tourists Fallacy.

Tourists also results in an expansion of the money supply without the creation of any more local debt. If we provide social dividends to the citizens we could get to enjoy our own tourist resorts.

The More Consumer Loans Fallacy.

The practice of issuing additional financial credit as consumer loans appears to solve some of the problem, in that at least some of the production is being consumed, however increasing debt burdens cause many social difficulties that are well documented. The methods of issuing this sort of credit are numerous. Leasing is a simple example: the goods are literally purchased by the bank and rented to the hapless lessee who becomes a slave to his lease payments. He has literally become an unwitting servant of mammon.

The Work Harder Fallacy.

Work harder producing what? Get a second job, producing more goods that can't be sold in a glutted market. Vance Packard in his classic book "The Waste Makers" provides graphic descriptions of the problem. He described, as I recall, that tyres produced by Olympic Tyres would last 100,000 miles but financially the company needed more tyre sales. They changed the tyres so they would only last 50,000 miles and soon solved their financial problem. Working hard to produce goods designed, it seems, to breakdown just after the warranty period expires is the logical outcome of an insane financial system. Working harder also means that an even higher proportion of our income is lost in taxes.

The Produce More Fallacy.

Why increase production when the problem is lack of consumption. Millions of dollars are spent on advertising to encourage sales of products without addressing the general shortage of purchasing power and problem of debt.

The Save More Money Fallacy.

Save more equals buy less. Savings represent unused purchasing power. Increased savings require reduced consumption, leaving more goods unsold.

The investment of savings in more production will create even more goods that cannot all be consumed either.　Investing savings in further production compounds the problem.

The Consume Less Fallacy.

The only legitimate purpose for production is consumption.　Consuming less of what is available, affordable and desired is pointless.　Advocating reduced consumption only makes sense because in the current financial system rewards designed obsolescence, which causes unnecessary waste products.

The Austerity Fallacy.

Nations and individuals are expected to adopt austerity policies and live within their financial means?　But the financial means are artificially scarce because of banker imposed policies designed to destroy the independence and freedom of people and nations.　If production is both physically practical and socially desirable then it can be made financially possible.　If private bankers are tricking people into austerity measures they are acting against the common good. The creators of our money supply are using their banking licences to deny citizens access to their own production.

If anyone playing banker in the game of Monopoly carried on like the commercial bankers are doing in real life they would have been kicked out of the game long ago.　It is time commercial bankers are prevented from playing the game of life by their own set of rules to the detriment of everyone else.

10. Solving the U.S.A.'s Debt Problem.

The U.S. Debt Clock (www.debt-clocks.com) recently showed the US National Debt as over fifteen trillion dollars, which comes to $49,500 per citizen. (Trillion = 1 million, million. Population is 313.3 million.)

Most citizens have been deceived into thinking of the debt as an amount that they somehow owe and are responsible to pay back, although they don't know how. No wonder the debt figures are thought of as rather daunting.

Fortunately there is another way of viewing the U.S., debt. More importantly the debt figures indicate how much money was created by the banks, claimed as their own and put into circulation as interest bearing loans. Most people think that the bankers want this money repaid as soon as possible. Bankers even contribute to this idea.

The truth is the bankers do not want debts repaid unless it politically suits them. Usually they reissue the credit, (roll over the debts) and this is because they just want everyone working for them, forever paying interest on credit the bankers create with computer entries that are made at no real cost to themselves.

The debts came into existence with the creation of credit, which enters circulation as various loans. If the debt was ever fully repaid, the interest burden yoke would be lifted from the community and the bankers' apparently valid claim to receive interest payment from the community would also cease. That is why bankers don't really want the principal repaid; just the interest... forever!

Looked at another way however, the total U.S. debt is the amount of money that needs to be created to repay the debt. The money to repay the debt doesn't need to be physically printed. Most importantly it must not be issued as interest bearing debt.

Consider this: Is it not true that any bank debt can be repaid by an issue of credit from any other bank? This is much the same as when banks offer "balance transfer" deals to customers. Newly issued credit from one bank wipes the old debt and its associated interest charges.

At the same time as the old debt is extinguished, the credit received is also extinguished from the books of the original debt holder. So the bank receiving the new credit doesn't get to spend it. The reason they don't get to spend it is because the credit they receive is cancelled out of existence when applied to the debt they hold. The asset value they held, which was really the "promise to pay" made by the borrower, is also redeemed.

The good thing about knowing the current debt per citizen is that it gives us a ball park figure indicating how much new credit needs to be issued and distributed democratically to all the citizens. The figure is almost exactly the amount that will be required so that there will eventually be enough new credit in circulation to repay the debt created by and owing to the banks.

By this simple process the creditors to the financial system will become the citizens rather than the commercial banks. Banks are non- living, soulless, abstract entities that have by deception usurped the ownership and benefits of owning the money supply from the people.

A way to understand the deception is to realize that the commercial banks authorize new deposits as they grant loans. The process of issuing each loan creates a bank asset, which is the Treasury bill or other loan document, signed by the borrower. The abstract credits the banks issue as loans create deposits in the banking system.

The paradigm shift is realizing that loans create deposits. Not the other way around as is commonly espoused.

A far more important matter to be considered is; who will get to own the newly created money; the interest and debt free credit that must be issued to cancel existing bank debts.

There are three main contenders;

- The bookkeepers, being the bankers who record the transactions and presently claim ownership over all new money, consisting of bank deposits and currency.

- The Government, who would love to control all the money (and consequently control all the people) or

- The citizens, who, along with their ancestors actually manufactured (past tense) the existing real wealth of the country.

Money functions as claim tickets on real wealth. Available real wealth determines the value of money.

The bankers currently claim all new credit as their own but without doubt, the only morally fair thing will be to issue the replacement stream of debt free credit equally to every citizen, rich and poor alike.

The astonishingly Good News is that the "per Citizen" figure accurately reveals the amount of new debt free money that will ultimately need to be issued and distributed, per citizen, to enable the repayment of the total bank debt, within the United States.

The rate of issue should at least match the rate that existing debts are being paid off. This way the new credit will top up the money supply and replace the deposits being cancelled out of existence by the ongoing repayment of existing debts.

It will be essential to raise the fractional reserve ratio to 100%, so that the commercial (trading) banks cannot multiply the new funds and arbitrarily inflate the money supply, which would cause inflation and would otherwise be used by the banks to discredit a national debt repayment program.

It would be appropriate to allocate some of the new money to subsidies of all local production. The subsidies should be applied at the consumers' end of the production system, as an aid to consumption, not at the producer end of the cycle because that can trigger unnecessary (unwanted) production.

Any State with its own State bank could and should issue payments of bank credit to its citizens. However, it would not be appropriate to have the State Bank issue credit direct to the State Government. Doing so would be a very dangerous practice because of the resulting centralization of power. State government funding will still come from taxes and borrowings from the citizens.

Taxes would still be levied for services because, in its purest form, a tax is a fee for services rendered. It is safer to provide the funds to the citizens and have the State justify its tax collections and borrowings to the electorate.

Under the present system, new debts come into existence when new credits (loans) are issued. Debts are further expanded when interest charges are added to existing loan accounts.

The reduction of total debt, let alone its elimination, is impossible using credit issued as interest bearing loans. Debt based credit (loans) can never reduce total debt. The present financial system is mathematically incapable of repaying the total debt without swallowing up the entire money supply and even then, there could still remain debt obligations pertaining to interest charges for which no credit has ever been issued.

The new financial credit (money) that must be issued for national debt replacement needs to be issued to all citizens equally. The credit must be free of interest, debt and tax.

Long term one can expect that the money supply will steadily increase, that is unless through natural disasters, war or lack of maintenance, the rate of creation of real wealth falls below the rate of consumption of real wealth. Then the money supply may need to be reduced to keep it accurately reflecting the physical economy.

11. An Offer to Bank Shareholders.

It is technically simple to correct the flaw in the banking system and fortunately the correction is in the best interest of almost everyone, including bank shareholders.

At present deposited funds are currently accounted for only as a liability in the banks' balance sheet.

The simplest way to bring bank shareholders on side with ideas in the Light Yoke is with an offer along the following lines.

The community may allow banks to credit their books with the asset value of funds deposited with them in exchange for a rise in the so called fractional reserve ratio to 100% and an agreement that banks will no longer issue bank credit.

Commercial trading banks will be allowed to store peoples' money or lend peoples' money but not both at the same time, as they currently pretend to do.

This offer will leave the asset value of bank loans as clear assets and would result in an immediate upward revaluation of bank shares.

Sure, banks will lose forever the right to create money out of nothing but in exchange the banks would legally gain heretofore undisclosed assets, the book value of funds deposited in the bank. Bank bookkeeping would come into line with that of all other businesses who must record both the asset and liability values of other peoples' money they hold in trust.

This proposal will also solve the bankers' problem of toxic assets, which currently threaten bank solvency. Toxic assets are the assets entered into their balance sheet as a result of bank credit issued as loans that will never be repaid. Sub-prime mortgages for example could easily include a large proportion of toxic assets.

With everyone in the community ready to benefit to the tune of tens of thousands of dollars and bank shareholders clear winners as well, it will be interesting to see who will oppose the proposals in the Light Yoke and why. In the long run the only people who are likely to oppose these proposals are those who wield the corrupt and substantially irresponsible power derived from the current banking system. These people however are few and readily identifiable. They may wisely choose to support the proposals, knowing that they can simply be out voted in shareholder meetings or outlawed in the legislature.

The proposals in the Light Yoke will do much to reduce both mortgage stress and minimise any need for the ruthless behaviour of banks in foreclosing on customers' homes and businesses. Bank behaviour can be better understood as an attempt to protect themselves from potential insolvency because of bad debts. Crediting banks with the asset value of their deposits will remove this fear and allow for more compassionate behaviour.

The corrupting influence of money will be dissipated amongst the citizens and the heavy yoke of bank debt will cease to exist.

THE LIGHT YOKE

Messianic Minister Ken (Malakai) Yeomans

March 1, 2012 Version 1.0114 5.5x8.5

P.O. Box 3289, Southport,

Queensland, 4215

AUSTRALIA

Mobile +61 4 1874 5120

Email: ken.yeomans@keyline.com.au

Skype: kenyeomans

Phone +61 7 5591 6281

Fax +61 7 5528 5977

The Light Yoke - Debunking Banking – How to remove the heavy yoke of bank debt with dividend payments to all citizens.

The cost burden of servicing bank debt is a heavy yoke on all societies that accept commercial trading bank credit as a valid addition to their money supply. In 1978 the Bank of NSW revealingly published that: "All money is a debt of the banking system." In other words all money is issued by commercial trading banks, claimed as their own and loaned at interest to borrowers. We are in effect using a rented money supply and there can be no end to the resulting debt. The real costs of using bank credit are corruption, inflation, higher taxation, austerity measures, war and the forced sale of personal and national assets.

Currently there are only three sources of money that can be used to repay bank debt. These are: new bank loans, current deposits and cash. New bank loans are commonly used to repay existing bank debts; but as bank credit is borrowed into existence, it automatically creates a corresponding debt so it is impossible for bank issued credit to ever reduce total debt.

Clearly an additional supply of credit needs to be put into circulation that isn't borrowed. This new money should be given to all the citizens and can be debt free, interest free and tax free. Just as citizens freely receive electoral votes as a right, so too regular dividend payments can and should be deposited into all citizens' accounts. In Australia the M3 money supply and matching bank debts are around $60,000 per person. So about $60,000 each is the amount that needs be issued to all citizens during the process of repaying total bank debt. Commercial trading banks can be prevented from reissuing bank credit by raising the fractional reserve ratio to 100% and in exchange they could be permitted to add the asset value of their deposits to their balance sheets.

Social credit dividends paid to all citizens are a fair and democratic way to decentralise the corrupting power of money and transform the heavy yoke of bank debt into the light yoke of economic freedom and a democratised money supply.